Also from Westphalia Press
westphaliapress.org

The Idea of the Digital University

Dialogue in the Roman-Greco World

The Politics of Impeachment

International or Local Ownership?: Security Sector Development in Post-Independent Kosovo

Policy Perspectives from Promising New Scholars in Complexity

The Role of Theory in Policy Analysis

ABC of Criminology

Non-Profit Organizations and Disaster

The Idea of Neoliberalism: The Emperor Has Threadbare Contemporary Clothes

Donald J. Trump's Presidency: International Perspectives

Ukraine vs. Russia: Revolution, Democracy and War: Selected Articles and Blogs, 2010-2016

Iran: Who Is Really In Charge?

Stamped: An Anti-Travel Novel

A Strategy for Implementing the Reconciliation Process

Issues in Maritime Cyber Security

A Different Dimension: Reflections on the History of Transpersonal Thought

Contracting, Logistics, Reverse Logistics: The Project, Program and Portfolio Approach

Unworkable Conservatism: Small Government, Freemarkets, and Impracticality

Springfield: The Novel

Lariats and Lassos

Ongoing Issues in Georgian Policy and Public Administration

Growing Inequality: Bridging Complex Systems, Population Health and Health Disparities

Designing, Adapting, Strategizing in Online Education

Secrets & Lies in the United Kingdom: Analysis of Political Corruption

Pacific Hurtgen: The American Army in Northern Luzon, 1945

Natural Gas as an Instrument of Russian State Power

New Frontiers in Criminology

Feeding the Global South

Beijing Express: How to Understand New China

Demand the Impossible: Essays in History as Activism

The Blue Friars

The Blue Friars: Their Sayings and Doings

Being a New Chapter in the History of Old Plymouth

W. H. K. Wright

Westphalia Press
An Imprint of the Policy Studies Organization
Washington, DC
2026

The Blue Friars, Their Sayings And Doings: Being A New
Chapter In The History Of Old Plymouth

All Rights Reserved © 2026
by Policy Studies Organization

Westphalia Press
An imprint of Policy Studies Organization
1527 New Hampshire Ave. NW
Washington, D.C. 20036
info@ipsonet.org

ISBN-13: 978-1-63723-651-2

Cover design by Jeffrey Barnes:
jbarnesbook.design

Daniel Gutierrez-Sandoval, Executive Director
PSO and Westphalia Press

Updated material and comments on this edition
can be found at the Westphalia Press website:
www.westphaliapress.org

THE BLUE FRIARS:

Their Sayings and Doings.

BEING

A NEW CHAPTER IN THE HISTORY OF OLD PLYMOUTH.

BY

W. H. K. WRIGHT, F.R. Hist. Soc.,

BOROUGH LIBRARIAN, PLYMOUTH.

With Portraits and other Illustrations.

London:
SIMPKIN, MARSHALL AND CO.

Plymouth:
W. FRANK WESTCOTT, Frankport Street.

1889.

In the interest of creating a more extensive selection of rare historical book reprints, we have chosen to reproduce this title even though it may possibly have occasional imperfections such as missing and blurred pages, missing text, poor pictures, markings, dark backgrounds and other reproduction issues beyond our control. Because this work is culturally important, we have made it available as a part of our commitment to protecting, preserving and promoting the world's literature. Thank you for your understanding.

PLYMOUTH:
Printed by W. FRANK WESTCOTT, at the Frankfort Press.

TABLE OF CONTENTS.

	PAGE
LIST OF ILLUSTRATIONS	v.
DEDICATION	vi.
PREFACE	vii., viii.
INTRODUCTION	1
"Blue Friar Pleasantries"—Introductory	4
Origin of the "Blue Friars"	9
Blue Friar Records	13
Canons of the Order	14, 19
Appointment of Lay Brethren	20
Capt. Nicholas Lockyer	24, 28
Election of a Blue Sister	25
Election of John Collier	27
Appointment of the Blue Cardinal	29
Lay Brother Robert Scanlan	31
Charles Mathews made a Blue Friar	32
Election of Sir Thomas Dyke Acland	36
Blue Friar Song	37
Election of Mr. William Eastlake	37
Death of Brother "Prism"	38
Election of Brother Glastonbury	39
Precept from the Cardinal	42
Brother Optimus	43
Blue Friar Pleasantries in *Fraser's Magazine*	44
Blue Friars' Sauce	46
Fines of the Order	48
Lay of St. Andrew's Bell	50
Death of the Cardinal	52
A Piteous Excuse	53
Visit of Queen Victoria	54
Specification for a Blue Friar Lodge	56
The Prior's Precept	57
Death of Mr. William Eastlake	59

iv.

Refectorial Programme in Latin	61
A Blue Friar Menu	62
The Treasurer's Accounts	64
Death of the Prior	66
Songs by Mr. William Jacobson	70-2
Death of Brother Bacon	73
Biographical Notice of Brother Locke	75
Anecdotes of Mr. Wightwick	77-8
Biographical Notes on Mr. John Collier	80
"The Lament"	81
The Poet Carrington	85
"The Private View"	86
The Late John Leech	88
Epistle to R. R. Scanlan	90
Blue Friar Canticles	92-3
Chronological Retrospect of Blue Friarism	99-111
"My Acquaintance with the late Charles Mathews"	112-30
Prismatic Reminiscences	131-40
Reminiscences of Liston	141-7
Lays in Praise of Soup—Introductory	148
,, ,, Origin of Mulligatawny Soup	149
,, ,, Gravy Soup	156
,, ,, Ox Tail Soup	159
,, ,, Pea Soup	161
On Knockers	165-9
Knockers *versus* House Bells	170-3
Some Account of the Natural and Artificial History of Corks	174-84
On Various Kinds of Sticks	185-8
Lubin's Log	189-96
"Popping the Question" according to Modern Experience	197-216
APPENDIX—Biographical Notice of Brother Roger (Mr. T. D. Newton); and Biographical Note of Brother Glastonbury (Mr. Edwin Lovell)	217, 218
List of Subscribers	219-24

LIST OF ILLUSTRATIONS.

	PAGE
Plan of a B. F. Lodge	*Frontispiece*
Seal of the Venerable Order of Blue Friars	5
B. F. Emblematical Ring	32
Portrait of Brother Prism (Charles Mathews)	*facing* 33
The B. F. Button	37
Label of the B. F. Sauce	47
Blue Friar Menu Card	*facing* 55
Portrait of the Prior (William Jacobson)	*facing* 67
Portrait of Brother Bacon (Sir W. Snow Harris)	*facing* 73
Portrait of Brother Locke (George Wightwick)	*facing* 75
Portrait of Brother Glastonbury (Edwin Lovell)	*facing* 97
Cast of the Hand of Charles Mathews	130
Portrait of Brother Prism in the character of "Sharp," in "The Lying Valet"	*facing* 131
Fac-simile of Play Bill—"Mr. Mathews at Home"	133
Portrait of Brother Roger (T. D. Newton)	*facing* 141
The Blue Box	216

Dedicated

(by permission)

TO

"YE SETTE OF ODD VOLUMES"

(H. J. GORDON ROSS, Esq., President)

*As a Society of Distinguished Men of Letters,
whose tastes and pursuits,
as well as their contributions to contemporary literature,
prove them to be kindred spirits
to the men whose " sayings and doings " are here
set forth in due order by the*

Chronicler of the "Blue Friars."

PREFACE.

FEW words are needed to introduce this little volume to the public, because, in the first place, the book tells its own tale, and secondly, the Introduction contains nearly all that can or need be said upon the matter. However, as it is the fashion of the times to pen "fore-words" to every volume which is not simply a work of fiction, of course the custom must be observed, though in truth little is left to say. A preface usually contains a *resumé* of the book itself, and thus saves the hard-working reviewer the time and labour which would be otherwise entailed by its perusal. But I may not offer my kind critics such immunity from the study of the following pages, and for their sakes will refrain from indicating in any way the *exact* character of the book. It is sufficient to mention that the first part of the "Blue Friars and their Sayings and Doings" is an expansion of a lecture delivered by me to the Members of the Plymouth Institution, at the Athenæum, on March 28th, 1889, and that the second portion includes several papers which have never before been published, and which for many years lay within the sacred recesses of a certain BLUE BOX whose quest had hitherto been in vain. Its selected contents are here set forth for the delight of the quizzical reader, through the kindness and courtesy of

Mr. Edwin Lovell Lovell, its fortunate possessor, who in the most generous manner has placed the whole of the papers at my disposal, with permission to use them in any way I please. To Mr. Lovell, therefore, my hearty thanks are due, and I can only regret that it is impossible to print in this little volume the twentieth part of the valuable and interesting material he has placed in my hands. For the present, let me express the hope that sufficient favour will be accorded to the Dicti of the Cerulean Brothers as to warrant the speedy addition of a second volume of "Pleasantries" culled from the stores of that chest they kept and loved so well.

I have also to thank Mrs. Wightwick for her very interesting notes relative to "Brother Locke"; and Mr. G. F. Radmore for the loan of several interesting MS. volumes of jottings, etc., of the late Prior of the Order. Further, I am indebted to many other correspondents for their interesting notes and reminiscences of the various members of the Venerable Order: to each and all my most sincere thanks are respectfully tendered.

Lastly, to my subscribers (whose names will be found at the end of the volume) let me offer my acknowledgments for their prompt and kindly encouragement— without which I should have hesitated at taking so bold a step as to publish the "Records" of a comparatively unknown fraternity.

W. H. K. WRIGHT.

Plymouth, Sept., 1889.

The Blue Friars.

INTRODUCTION.

THE town of Plymouth can boast of the existence of at least three Monastic establishments within its walls in early days, these being connected respectively with the three religious orders known as the White Friars, or Carmelites, the Grey Friars, or Franciscans, and the Black Friars, or Dominicans. Of the first of these, the memory is still kept alive by street names, such as Friary Street, Whitefriars Street, and Whitecross Street, situated near or within the lands formerly occupied by them, and of which the Friary Station is now about the centre. Similarly the Black Friars, whose location appears to have been near Southside Street, have their name perpetuated in Blackfriars' Lane; the distillery of Messrs. Coates and Company having undoubtedly been a portion of their religious house. Of the Franciscans or Grey Friars not even the name remains. Their house was situated in Woolster Street, and a portion of it was converted into an inn—the Mitre Tavern—but this has been lately demolished. To those who would know more of the history of these notable religious fraternities, we would recommend the perusal of the two histories of Plymouth, by Mr. R. N. Worth, and the late Mr. Llewellynn Jewitt, respectively, where ample details will be found. Another work which deals exhaustively with this feature of local history, entitled, *The Ecclesiastical History of Old Plymouth*, by Mr. J. Brooking Rowe, will also be found most instructive.

We have now to deal with an entirely different kind of fraternity, of whom little or nothing is said in either of the works we have enumerated, for obvious reasons, which will be hereafter particularized. The silence of our local historians as to the doings of the Blue Friars may be due to the fact that their proceedings were of a somewhat mysterious and secret character, and that the record of those proceedings was until recently in private hands, and was not within reach of the writers of the historical works named. Or it may be that the learned Plymouth historians deigned not to consider such particulars as could be gleaned concerning the Venerable Order of Blue Friars of sufficient interest or importance to be incorporated in their works. We venture to think otherwise, and, by a lucky accident having obtained most reliable information concerning this notable brotherhood, we have determined to impart the same to the public through the following pages, and thus to furnish an additional chapter to local history.

Our readers will be able to judge for themselves, by a perusal of this little volume, whether our estimate of the value of these details is a just one, and whether the information herein contained is worthy of their attention, and the sayings and doings of the Blue Friars worthy of being chronicled in a separate volume.

We would first undeceive our readers as to the relation these Blue Friars bore to the other monastic orders which flourished in Old Plymouth. The Blue Friars were not a religious order: they dwelt not in a monastery, they were not sworn to celibacy: they did not forswear the good things of life, nor forego its enjoyments and pleasures. On the contrary, they were men of mirth and wisdom; men whose words and opinions were of considerable weight with their fellows: for although much of their wisdom has been lost, enough remains to prove that they shed a lustre upon society in the times in which they lived, and that they have left behind them in their writings (some of which are here gathered for the delectation of the curious) enduring monuments of their genius.

Before proceeding to give a detailed and, we trust, fairly accurate record of the doings of the Blue Friars, we purpose quoting the introductory chapter to a series of papers entitled *Blue Friar Pleasantries*, which appeared in *Fraser's Magazine* some fifty years ago, containing most witty and apposite remarks upon the origin of the Order.

We shall also include in our little volume some of the most interesting and amusing of the *Pleasantries* themselves, besides giving a few biographical particulars of the most prominent members of the Order, and such other information as we may be able to gather during the progress of the work through the press.

Blue Friar Pleasantries.

NO. I.—INTRODUCTORY.

Published in *Fraser's Magazine*, 1837, Vol. 1, p. 223.

"*I feel now the future in the instant.*"—SHAKESPEARE.

It is well known (but the anecdote is good enough to be again repeated) that the attempt once made to stimulate an Irishman's ambition by a reference to posthumous fame, was met by the reply, " Why should I do anything for posterity ? Posterity never did anything for me."

The Blue Friars, however, who have an equal power with Macbeth's witches to look into futurity, are by no means in the Irishman's case ; for, unless they are much mistaken, they clearly see, as a thing already done, what posterity will do for them, and are duly grateful.

Their modesty will not suffer them to transcribe all that the discriminating critic of the future is pleased to say in their eulogy; but they are amused with his speculations as to the origin and nature of the brotherhood, and as to the who and what of the Blue Brothers individually.

The B.F.'s, therefore, saying nothing themselves on these heads, are content to let posterity speak for them ; and, accordingly, posterity thus speaks :—

"*Researches concerning the Monastic Orders of Great Britain, from the earliest times until the final extinction of the celebrated Order of Blue Friars, in the nineteenth century. Dated* 2836."

(Extracts from pages 406, 410, and 411.)

" About this time—one thousand years back—we first hear of that order of wisdom, wit, and good fellowship,

whose members were the authors of those volumes of *pleasantrie*, which are among the most val— * *
* * * * * * *
* * * times, ancient or modern."

The foregoing hiatus supplies the place of pages 407, 8, and 9, which are replete with commendations not to be hoped for from contemporary critics. The antiquarian thus proceeds:—

"The origin of the Blue Order is involved in obscurity; though writers have been found determinate in the belief that it was forest-born with Robin Hood and his merry men. The reader will instantly see an objection to this in the fact of Robin's having been a *green*—and not a *blue*—man; but even this discrepancy is met with an explanation by Professor Grubdust, whose hypothesis chiefly rests on what he imagines to be a true decipherment of the monastic seal, still fortunately preserved to us, and a copy of which is here adjoined.

It is said that the letters W. H. I. N. form a decided word; and, certainly, there *is* such a word, exactly so spelt, and put down in the dictionary as a noun-substantive, signifying *furze*, *shrub*, *prickly-bush*. Professor Grubdust thence deduces his conclusion that the brethren frequented heaths, commons, or woods; that they were originally huntsmen, or highwaymen,—"night's foresters," as signified by the owl,—merrymen by day, as typified by the magpie,—alternately fierce and funny, as shewn by the double-headed crest (the profiles of which relatively indicate the ferocity of their high-way maraudings, and the fun of their indoor revelries),—that the "nos nostra-que" denotes their corporate interests, and that the clasped

hands mean nothing more than "honour among thieves,"
—that they *were* green brothers, until the dissolution of
monasteries in the time of Harry the Eighth, after which
they became blue—because they had good reason to look
so. The professor further believes, that with the change
of their coats they also changed the habit of their minds,
and subsequently became mere innocent freebooters in
the whims and oddities of humanity, the fruits of their
gatherings being now before the world in their volume
of " Pleasantries."

Professor Mustyhead reads the seal differently, and
gives it as his opinion, that the Blue Brothers have never
been false to the colours which they originally nailed to
their mast; that, although exclusive as it respects their
monasticism, they were philanthropic in regard to the
practical good which emanated therefrom; and that they
could alternately chatter with the magpie or philosophise
with the owl. " Then," says he, " look at the double-
headed crest, with ' cinnamon and ginger ' in the one
face, and wisdom and water-gruel in its fellow—exempli-
fying that exact medley of jollity and asceticism which
should distinguish every mortal, who, with good cause to
be merry to-day, can yet say, with Mercutio, ' ask for me
to-morrow, and you'll (perhaps) find me a *grave* man.' "
The four mysterious letters are translated by Mustyhead
into Wisdom, Hilarity, Innocence, and Noodledum,—
shewing how the wise, the happy, and the innocent, may
consistently indulge in a few occasional freaks of fantasy
not exactly appertaining to the philosophy of mind.
Professor Threadbare supports an opinion, that W.H.I.N.
are the initials of Will, Harry, Jack, and Nathaniel; but
with less reason than he might adduce in proof that they
stand for Wine, Harrico, Jelly, and Nutcrackers. Others
incline to the belief, that the four letters are the initials
of the founders' names; and, certes, as they say, B.F.

may signify *Brothers Four* as well as Blue *Friars*. But B.F. *may* also signify *Brothers Fifty*,—leaving us to conclude that the fraternity is of heathen origin, being descended from the fifty sons of Ægyptus, who got their throats cut—" all save one "—by marrying the Danaides.

For our own parts, we incline to believe that they comprised a fraternity which associated under the patronage of "two-headed Janus," by whom they swore, as the merry Gratiano instructed them; and that they held themselves free to laugh at a jest, without caring a whit whether Nestor deemed it laughable or not: that they were in the habit of holding periodical conclaves, when, under the invigorating influence of the wassail-bowl, each brother delivered an essay on men, manners, and things; and that from the collection of papers thus made, were subsequently selected those which we now possess under the title of

"BLUE FRIAR PLEASANTRIES."

Concerning the individuals who comprised the fraternity, we know little more than is to be gathered from the signatures of those whose contributions have been published to the world. These are observed to be as follow:—*Herricke* (the cardinal), *Tuck* (the prior), *Locke*, (sub-prior), *Bacon*, *Somno*, *Prism*, *Glastonbury*, and *Roger* (sacristan). Of these, Tuck, Locke, Roger, and Bacon are, on two occasions, alluded to as "*the* four" distinct from the others,—leaving us to imagine that the fraternity at one time consisted of these only, and, at all events, making it certain that *they* were contemporaneous.

In Locke's poem of the "Bridal Banquet" we have the following :—

" Such glint'ning eyes and habits gay
As on this Hymeneal day
Have sure been seen by few :
The bravest knight and fairest dame

> Were seen to head the line; then came
> A hundred guests of honoured fame,
> And *four*, at last, of worthiest name,—
> God bless the Brothers Blue!"

Again :—

> "The twain are gone—my song is o'er,—
> The guests have parted—save *the four*:
> They entered last of all the rout—
> They'll be the last to vanish out;
> For, ere they go, they must unthrottle
> The neck of many a balsam-bottle,
> And spice with many a joke their liquor,
> And sing a 'fico for the vicar.'
> And if, when Sol the morn shall greet,
> They're found not *on* the banquet-seat,
>   With caps and noses red,
> Then look below upon the ground,
> And if they may not *there* be found
>   'Tis like they're gone to bed.
> And so, good night, Sir Prior Blue,—
> Roger, Bacon, Locke, adieu!"

Whether these were the *original* or the *surviving* "four," must be left open to discussion, together with a variety of other indications which may be gathered from a careful perusal of the B.F. Miscellány. It is, however, clearly ascertained, that at one happy period of the monastery's existence the celebrated Charles Mathews (who stood *alone* in the comic department of the drama) was its most distinguished member. This fact is expressly recorded in a sketch of the last days of the Hogarthian actor, penned by one of his Blue Brothers, and first issued to the world by James Fraser, of well-beloved memory, under the title of 'My Acquaintance with the late Charles Mathews.' His actual name not appearing among the autograph signatures, leaves us to presume that the brethren, on their admission into Blue Orders, were invested with certain cognominations independent of those given to them by their godfathers and godmothers; nor is it improbable that 'Brother Prism' was no other than the monastic appellation of the *prismatic* minded Mathews, through whom, as an optical medium, the world saw itself in all its multiformity."

We are content to let the foregoing stand as it is. There is "no offence in it," at least. Perhaps our contemporary readers will regard it as "much ado about nothing;" nor will we hazard the chance of making that "much" *more*.

𝔏𝔬𝔠𝔨𝔢.

From our Cerulean Cell, this 15th January, 1837.

So much, then, for the introduction to the Pleasantries, which, it must be confessed, does not throw much light upon the subject, the intention of the writer having been merely to indulge in a little harmless fun, and to surround his history with mystery. It is now our duty and privilege to remove the veil which has for so many years hung over the Blue Friars and their doings, and to dispel any mystery which may yet attach to them.

There lately came into the possession of the writer of this book several volumes of MS., containing "Records of the Order of Blue Friars," together with sundry papers written by one of their number. In one of these volumes appears the following memorandum in the handwriting of Friar Tuck (the Prior) which briefly explains the origin of the Order:—

"Between twenty and thirty years ago it was agreed by myself and three friends during a delightful day in the country, that we should meet once in a quarter of a year to enjoy a pic-nic in the summer months, and in the winter season to dine at each other's houses. The name of a Club was rejected, and after some discussion it was agreed that we should dub ourselves 'Blue Friars,' the reason of which you may hereafter hear. Each member was to produce at each meeting an original paper, under forfeiture of a dozen of wine for any omission. This book (referring to the manuscript book in which this memorandum appears) contains some of my contributions which, mostly, from that time to the present have remained uncorrected, a fact that you cannot fail to perceive. We were originally, as I have stated, four members only, but subsequently two others were added to our number; the Rev. J. H. Macaulay, a relative of the writer of the *History of England*, and the late Charles Mathews. Our meetings were more assimilated to boys let out for a holiday than any other thing with which I can compare them."

The Society or Brotherhood was thus founded in the year 1829, and its original members were, Mr. William Jacobson (the writer of the note quoted above), who was a solicitor of considerable eminence in Plymouth, and chiefly instrumental in founding the Small Debts Court, which afterwards became the County Court: he was a highly accomplished gentleman; one who is remembered with great respect by many of the older members of the Plymouth Institution, of which he was a distinguished member. His portrait hangs on the walls of the Art Gallery in the Athenæum. Another member was Mr. George Wightwick, a well-known architect, also resident in Plymouth. His skill in his profession, as well as his high ability in the histrionic art, coupled with his gentlemanly bearing and great hospitality, made him a favourite in cultured circles during the whole period of his residence in the town; and on his removal to Clifton he was the recipient of some substantial tokens of esteem, to which, with other particulars, we shall refer in a later portion of this book. The other members were Mr. William Snow Harris (afterwards knighted for his scientific researches and discoveries), an eminent surgeon; and Mr. T. Duncan Newton, who although a member of the original *four*, does not appear to have possessed any great capabilities either as an entertainer or a humorist. He was, however, a giver of good dinners, a very hilarious man, and was useful to the fraternity, as being the butt of the other members. Such were the original *four*, but there were others elected from time to time, as the "Records" will show, some of whom had far more than a local reputation. These men, with others, who will be enumerated hereafter, were among the leading spirits of the literary and professional life of Plymouth fifty years ago; they occupied prominent positions in the town, as well as at the Plymouth Institution: in its early days more of a centre of "light and leading" even than it is now.

It was the fancy of these men to form themselves into this small and select literary and convivial Club, and, in the performance of their self-imposed duties, to hold periodical conclaves at the houses of each in succession, there to dine, to crack jokes, to read papers original or selected, and to while away the hours in "the feast of reason and the flow of soul."

They were habited in a monkish dress of coarse serge with a hempen girdle, breeches and yellow stockings. Their dinner table was laid in a manner befitting their peculiar profession, its furniture and garniture being of a quaint and antique character. A stuffed owl and a magpie occupied positions of honour at each end of the table (as representatives of wisdom and hilarity), the centre being occupied with an alabaster salt-cellar. The chief dish on the table not unfrequently contained a strange mixture of viands. Wooden platters and pewter spoons were a not incongruous element in their monastic banquet, as doubtless their wine was none the less exhilarating if quaffed out of queer old-fashioned goblets which had done duty in many a bygone feast.

Altogether these gatherings, with their strange blending of mystery and jocularity, were events worth remembering, and but for the fact that, with rare exceptions, servants were prohibited from seeing or hearing these revels, much more of an entertaining character might have been made known to the outer world.

We have several times mentioned the " Records " of this Order. The " Blue Book " containing these " Records " came recently into our possession, and having previously known something of the fraternity from one who had close personal intercourse with them, we determined to incorporate these " Records " in a book, which should hand down to futurity the doings and some of the sayings of these notable men.

We propose to print the more interesting portions of these " Records," as the best means of giving the history of the Order, and of preserving the memorials of the " Blue Friars."

Blue Friar Records.

"The Book of the Records of the Blue Friars"
Contains an account of all their doings from the establishment of the Order in the year 1829 down to the year 1846, when it appears to have been dissolved. On the first page appears the following statement:
"The Order of Blue Friars was founded by us—

    Friar Tuck,   Friar Locke,
    Friar Bacon,   Friar Roger,

on the seventeenth day of May, in the Year of Our Lord One Thousand Eight Hundred and Twenty-nine, and in the Tenth Year of the reign of His Majesty George the Fourth."

Then follow sundry Canons, "instituted by us in full Conclave, on the twentieth day of July, 1829, for the observance of the Order of Blue Friars. To these and such other Canons as may at any time hereafter be made by us touching the above Order, we severally pledge ourselves to yield implicit obedience, to the extent of our power.

    By the hand of a Blue Friar.
                      [The Blue Friar Oath.]

    Signed—Tuck (the Prior).
               Locke (Sub-Prior).
               Bacon.
               Roger."

It may be as well here to state, in order that the reader may be able to identify the various personages as we proceed, that Tuck (the Prior), was Mr. Jacobson; Locke (Sub-Prior), Mr. Wightwick; Bacon, Mr. Harris; and Roger, Mr. Newton.

The following are the Canons to which reference is made above:—

"Canons.

"1. That for the first Twelve months, beginning on this twentieth day of July, 1829, and ending on the twentieth day of July, 1830, or last Quarterly Conclave, the Founders of the Order be elected to the following Offices, viz.:—

Prior	The Venerable Father Tuck.
Sub-Prior	Brother Locke.
Clerke	Brother Bacon.
Sacristan	Brother Roger.

The respective duties of which Offices are to be borne alternately by each of the Brethren, in yearly rotation, according to priority of birth.

"2. That cordiality, good fellowship, and brotherly love be the basis on which all proceedings of the Order be founded, and that their emblem be a Circle—the symbol of Eternity.

"3. That the objects of discussion at the various Meetings of the Brethren be, in the most unlimited sense, *de omnibus rebus cum multis aliis*, provided always that the same be not carried on dry-lipped.

"4. That a Grand Conclave of the Order be held in every year, on the following days, or as near thereto as conveniently may be, viz., the twentieth day of July, the twentieth day of October, the twentieth day of January, and the twentieth day of April, at 5 of the clock in the afternoon, on which occasions each Brother in rotation, and according to priority in monastic rank, shall receive the Fraternity in his Refectory, and provide for their bodily sustenance a Repast consisting of the following Items:—Soup or Fish, Beefsteaks or a plain Joint of Meat, Vegetables, and a Tart or Pudding. Any addition to this Refectory Catalogue shall subject the Brother so offending to such penance as the Prior for the time being may be pleased to enjoin. That at every such Grand Conclave, it is imperative, all excuses apart, that each of the Brethren do appear in the full costume of the Order, viz., a Blue Coat and Buff Kerseymere Vest with the B.F. buttons, a Blue Silk Belt and Black Neckerchief, Night-caps, Noses, B.F. Snuff-boxes, and such other additional Monastic paraphernalia, as may from time to time be determined on. The nether monk may be indued according as best beseemeth the respective fancy of each Brother. That in order to the effectual correction of all bad habits it be held incompetent for any Brother to be present at the Grand Quarterly Conclaves but in strict accordance with the foregoing regulations.

"5. That at every Grand Quarterly Conclave, immediately after the repast, the Records and Accounts of the Clerke and Sacristan be examined, audited and passed, and such other Monastic business transacted as may be necessary. On the completion of which each Brother is to produce and read to the Fraternity an original paper of his own composition, to be written on any subject, and treated of in any manner most agreeable to himself. Such original papers, together with any other compositions of pen or pencil, emanating from a Blue Friar, and approved in Conclave, to be deposited in a Box to be provided and kept for that purpose by the Clerke for the time being. That if any Brother shall at any of the Grand Quarterly Conclaves omit to furnish such original paper as aforesaid, he shall forfeit One Dozen Bottles of Friar's Balsam for the use and benefit of the Fraternity.

"6. That from time to time, to be determined on hereafter, a pamphlet be published by the Fraternity, to be called, *Transactions of the Blue Friars*, consisting of such selections from the Blue Box aforesaid as may be deemed advisable, embellished with lithographic sketches.

"7. That as opportunity may occur and circumstances permit, the Brotherhood do collect such Books and other Articles as may be considered worthy of preservation, to form the foundation of a Blue Library and Museum.

"8. That each Brother do now deposit in the hands of Brother Roger, the Sacristan, the sum of 30s., to meet the current expenses of the Order.

"9. That a record of all the proceedings of the Blue Friars be entered in a Book by the Clerke for the time being, to be read at the then next Grand Quarterly Conclave."

The next entry in the Records states that, "In consequence of the unfavourable state of the weather, and other unavoidable circumstances, the 'Rambles' of the 'Blue Friars' were not very numerous during the Summer of 1829, the only campaigns worthy of record taking place on May 18th and June 12th.

On 18th May, the Brethren, with the exception of Brother Locke, visited the Monastery on Mount Batten, celebrated their orgies round a roaring fire, and had a narrow escape of being sent to the Hulks for a breach of the Revenue Laws, the Officers of that Department considering this effort on the part of the Brethren to signalize themselves in a *spiritual calling* as more applicable to Smugglers than Monks." What 'Monastery' is referred to we can only imagine. It may have been a hospitable tavern.

On 12th June the Brethren performed a pilgrimage to Sheepstor, and consecrated certain portions of Land and

Water in that neighbourhood after their own fashion. The weather was in keeping with the occasion, and the day throughout was spent in the veriest zest of Blue Friarship. On this occasion the service of Plate, Chalices, &c., &c., appertaining to the Blue Refectory, were used for the first time—the Beefsteaks were broiled on a gridiron invented by Brother Bacon; contributions of Fuel were levied on the lay Impropriators of the soil —and though a hint from one of the Brethren as to having "*rather* mixed our Liquors" might suggest an Idea that we "*stood not* upon the order of our going," yet "the Feast of Reason and the Flow of Soul" was, strictly speaking, unsullied by Intemperance.

The next entry records the proceedings at the "First Grand Quarterly Conclave," held at the Refectory of the Venerable Prior, Father Tuck (Mr. Jacobson*), on the 20th July, 1829. On this occasion the several Canons hereinbefore recorded were instituted, and a contribution of 30s. from each of the Brethren, deposited in the hands of the Sacristan. On the completion of the business of yᵉ monastery, the following original papers were produced and read:—

The Prior: "Some Account of a Barbarous Murder lately committed at Plymouth."†

Brother Locke: "On the Ancient Drama."
Brother Bacon: "On Belief."
Brother Roger: "On being bothered."

According to an ancient monastic custom (a Record of which is preserved in the Blue Box) the Prior presented

---

* Probably at his residence, No. 8 Frankfort Street.

† This doubtless had reference to some Hoe improvements, as we have in our possession several Papers written by Mr. Jacobson, in which he expresses his strong disapproval of the measures then being taken by the Corporation for the alteration and improvement of this delightful spot.

each of the Brethren with six Flasks of "Friar's Balsam,"* to be used on such occasions only as all the Brethren meet together, but more especially at the Quarterly Conclaves. This custom is expected to be kept up by each Brother on his arriving at the dignity of Prior.

The following is a copy of the Record here referred to:—

"Extract from a Book lately discovered to have belonged to the Venerable Order of Blue Friars, and miraculously preserved upon the dissolution of monasteries by Henry the Eighth:—

"Andde theyre existethhe a certainne olde andde exceedygge auncient customme tyme outte off mynnde thatte the Superyoure of thyss order shall once in each yearre atte the leastte presentte untoe hys Brethrenne VI flaskes of wynne off ryghtte excellent quality, for the especialle comfortte of the Brethrenne durynge the dispatche off theirre monastic affaires and concernnes, which experience informeth us make large demandes upon the brainnes and require thatte the bodie shall be cheeredde withhe suitable potationnes."

Four figures of different monastic orders were presented from a Layman and accepted.

Some books were also presented by the Brethren, to remain in the keeping of the Prior, as the foundation of a Blue Library: but the list of books was omitted to be entered in the "Records" as was originally intended. The frequent references to the "Blue Box" and its interesting and varied contents, render it a subject of supreme regret that all trace of the whereabouts of this valuable receptacle of Blue Friar lore has been lost.†

---

* Query, Port Wine.

† Since writing the above we have discovered the Blue Box and these missing documents, about which we shall have something to say towards the end of this volume, besides being enabled by the valuable materials placed in our hands to include several original papers not previously published, and to illustrate these "Records" with many interesting notes.

The second Quarterly Conclave was held on the 11th December, 1829, at the Refectory* of the Sub-Prior, Brother Locke (Mr. Wightwick), on which occasion Aubrey Bizzi, Edwin Lovell, and Donald Barclay were elected Lay Brethren of the Order of Blue Friars, subject to the following Canon :—

"CANON 10.

"That all Lay Brethren, from the date of their respective appointments, be admitted to the enjoyment of all privileges now appertaining to the Order of Blue Friars, with the exception of being present at the Grand Quarterly Conclaves, to which, however, the founders have power to invite them, provided their consent be unanimous. Moreover, that Lay Brethren are to consider themselves in all things and at all times amenable to such Canons as now are and may hereafter be instituted by the Founders of the Order, as far as the same may be considered to relate to a Blue Layship."

We have been unable to discover the identity of Mr. Aubrey Bizzi and Mr. Barclay. Mr. Lovell afterwards became a full member of the Order, and its latest survivor. He was well known in Plymouth at the time, but not a resident. The Blue Book of the Records now in the possession of the writer, was his property, and was sold at a sale of effects at Sharcombe House, Dinder, near Wells, on February 28th, 1887. But of this and him more anon. The following original papers were then read :—

The Prior: "On the Legend of Jacky Horner."
Locke: "On the Seven Ages of Man."
Bacon: "A Thing of Shreds and Patches."
Roger: "On the Skiey Influences."

" Brother Locke then presented each of the Fraternity

---

* Athenæum Terrace.

with a snuff-box, ornamented with the emblem of the Order, and a blue silk belt from the Incip. Sister Blue the Sub-Prioress [Mrs. Wightwick], both of which were ordered thenceforth to form part of the Monastic paraphernalia, and to be produced by each brother at the Quarterly Conclaves." Mrs. Wightwick always supported her husband on these occasions with great hospitality, although she was not allowed to be present at the Conclaves.

Nothing special transpired at the third Quarterly Conclave held on February 5th, 1830, at the Refectory of Brother Bacon (Mr. Harris), the following being the papers then produced and read:—

The Prior: " A Merry Christmas."
Locke: " The Venus de Medici."
Bacon: " A Divertimento for a post chaise."
Roger: " On Knockers."

But at the following Meeting held on April 20th of the same year, at the Refectory of Brother Roger (Mr. Newton), some important business was transacted, which we quote *in extenso* from the "Records." At this meeting the appointments of Edwin Lovell and Donald Barclay as Lay Brethren of the Order were executed in due form, and delivered to the Prior to be transmitted to the parties concerned.

The following form of the appointment of a Lay Brother was ordered to be entered among the Blue Records, and to be used hereafter on all similar occasions:—

Form of appointment to a Blue Layship:

"Tuck, Locke, Bacon, and Roger, by the Bonds of good fellowship, of the United Hemispheres of Sense and Nonsense, Fixed Stars—of the Order of Blue Friars, Founders—Haters of Humbug, Defenders of Mirth, &c.,

&c. To our Trusty and Well-beloved———of———greeting.

"KNOW YE, That we in much estimation of your manifold good qualities, and for divers other reasons, us thereunto especially moving, Have appointed, and by these presents Do appoint you the aforesaid———to be a Lay Brother of our said Order of Blue Friars—and we do hereby admit and entitle you to the enjoyment of all and singular the privileges appertaining unto the said Order aforesaid (the knowledge of the mysteries of the four Grand Quarterly Conclaves always excepted and reserved) To which end you the aforesaid———are hereby required to swear 'By the hand of a Blue Friar' that you will at all times and places, ceasing every excuse, yield due and unlimited obedience to all such Canons as now are or hereafter may be instituted by us for the governance of the said Order so far as the same concern a Lay Brother. In default of which at any time you shall hereby pledge yourself to pay a forfeit to the Refectory of the said Order of One dozen bottles of Wine (the same to be tasted and approved by the Prior for the time being before receipt thereof) or submit to such other penalty as the Prior for the time being may be pleased to enjoin.

"Given at the cell of Prior Tuck the———day of ———18———in the———year of our Foundation. As Witness our Hands and the Minor Seal of the said Order.

   Tuck (L.S.), *Prior*. Bacon (L.S.)
   Locke (L.S.)   Roger (L.S.)"

The original papers read at this Conclave were as follows:—

The Prior: "Recollections of the Old Theatre at Plymouth."

Locke: "On Cicisbeism."

Bacon: "Illustrations of the Newtonian Philosophy."
Roger: "On the Generation of Vipers."

A copy of the first of these papers is in one of the MS. books now in the possession of the writer, and as it contains very interesting reminiscences and is quite worthy of publication, it will be included with the "Blue Friar Pleasantries" in the present volume. Another Canon was instituted at this meeting of a rather important character, which runs as follows:—

"CANON II.

"That from henceforth on the application of any of the Brethren to the Clerke for the time being for the loan of any papers deposited in the Blue Box, except those of his own composition, the said Clerke is interdicted from complying with such requests without the written consent of the author of such papers."

Then follows this interesting entry:—

"In consequence of the manifold arduous duties which devolve on Brother Bacon (Harris) in the course of his Philosophical investigations, Brother Roger was elected to the Office of Clerke *in perpetuam*—in conjunction with his former office of Sacristan."*

At this Conclave the Blue Box was consecrated, the papers and records deposited in it, and the whole ordered to remain in the custody of Brother Roger the Clerk. The best thanks of the Brethren were unanimously voted to Thomas Edwin Gosling for the beautiful manner in which he has embellished the said box with the emblems of the Order.†

On the conclusion of the business of the Monastery,

---

* We find that the Book of the "Records" is entirely in the handwriting of Brother Roger.

† The history of the Blue Box and its varied and interesting contents will be found in another part of this work.

Brother Bacon entertained the Conclave with a magnificent phantasmagoric exhibition.

The next meeting (August 31st, 1830) has nothing of particular interest except that " Brother Bacon furnished the Fraternity with a Box of Paddy's Mixture.* The Recollections of the Old Theatre were continued by the Prior, and Brother Locke contributed a paper, entitled ' The Hoeiad.'"

The Prior's Precept for holding this Conclave runs as follows :—

> "KNOWN BE IT (to rub off the rust)
> That Tuesday next, the thirty-first,
> Flesh and Fish will grace the board
> Of Friar Tuck—the choicest hoard
> Shall Balsam render *quantum suff.*,
> To cheer the lads of Blue and Buff.
> O Brothers Blue—Cerulean Friars,
> Attend the synod at thy Prior's;
> To plodders leave commercial jobs,
> And both with feigned and natural nobs,
> Whose tint alone exceeds the caps
> That fit your precious scalps like wax—
> Bring with you, every man, his paper,
> O'er which has wasted midnight taper—
> Come, be the weather fair or foul,
> Or, by my emblem fit, the Owl,
> By spoonsful sorrow shall ye suck—
> This swear I—your superior,
>
> TUCK.

From my inmost Cell,
   Aug. 27th, 1830."

We now come to an incident in the history of the brotherhood a little out of the ordinary run, in that it introduces us to a gentleman who was of no mean repute in his day and generation.

On September 20th, 1830, it is thus recorded :—
" The Fraternity this day undertook a voyage by sea

---
* Query, Taddy's Mixture.

for the purpose of inspecting the state of one of their Fisheries at the Laira Sands. It was discovered in a very untidy *pickle*, and marvellously unproductive of any *nett* produce. By the unanimous invitation of the Order, Capt. Nicholas Lockyer—the Mayor-elect of our good Town and Borough of Plymouth, undertook the command of the expedition. The Brethren then adjourned to their Monastery of Mount Batten and satisfied the inner man with their usual frugality and temperance; after which the Prior was graciously pleased to confer on the said Nicholas Lockyer for his arduous services while commanding the expedition, the degree of ' a Hap-hazard-out-of-door Blue Friar,' with permission to wear a buff waistcoat, decorated with the Buttons of the Order. The same honour was also conferred on William Lockyer, Comptroller of our Customs at Plymouth, and they took the oaths in that case made and provided. The joviality and good fellowship of the Brethren received no interruption from anything animate or inanimate during the day!" And then follows this highly characteristic, if somewhat slangy phrase—" Bakky Galore!"

The Sixth Quarterly Conclave was held on Oct. 20th, 1830, at the Refectory of the Sub-Prior, Brother Locke, on which occasion, by the special permission of the Prior, and by the general consent of the Fraternity, Lay Brother Edwin (Lovell) was permitted to be present at the celebration of such mysteries as might appertain to the above Conclave.

"A contribution of £1 from each of the Brethren was placed in the hands of the Sacristan for the general expenses of the Order. Brother Edwin presented to the Order a canister of Snuff (Old Paris) from the cellar of our ever-to-be-deplored brother, George the Fourth, which they were most graciously pleased to receive *nos[e] nostra que.*"

"In addition to the usual Refectory Items, a contribution of Blancmange from Sister Jane of the Crescent was admitted, under a dispensation from the Prior, and the general thanks of the Order transmitted to her for her kind present (she was *ipso facto* elected a Blue Sister. During the Conclave the Order received a visit from a Nun of the Ursuline Order,—an ambassadress from Doctor Williams, a Layman. She was graciously received and entertained at the charges of the Fraternity."

The following letter (apparently of introduction) found amongst the miscellaneous papers in the Blue Box, partially explains this unexpected visit :—

"The Mère St. George,
To the Brethren called
the Blue Friars,
S. P. D.

Having received permission from the Mère Superieure of the Convent of the Ursulines instituted at Montreal, in 1639, to visit foreign climes, I have made Plymouth a principal object of attention, and learning that a Meeting of the Cerulean Brethren was this evening to take place, I have determined to introduce myself to them —the more particularly, as this day being a *jour maigre*, I was perfectly certain that no food save the simplest fish, with the vegetable called the potatoe, would be introduced, and that no vinous potation could occur during the self-denying refection; the simple element alone being admissible.

As the streets may be infested by midnight revellers, I desire the protection of Brother Tuck to conduct me safely to my dwelling."

Several papers were read which need not be here enumerated; after which Brother Bacon presented the Fraternity with an account of a humorous Trial of a Patlander, illustrated by original drawings, which was graciously received and ordered to be placed among the archives of the Order.*

---

* These drawings are very funny, and the dialogue full of witty and smart sayings. We regret that they cannot be reproduced here.—ED.

The next entry, March 30th, 1831, records that "Lay Brethren Nicholas and William [Lockyer], met at the cell of Brother Bacon, in the evening, for the purpose of 'astonishing the natives,' or, in common parlance, eating oysters; Brother Edwin having sent a Barrel of the aforesaid shell-cocknies for the amusement of the fraternity. The thanks of the Order were unanimously voted to Brother Edwin for his donation."

"1831: April 14. The Seventh Quarterly Conclave was held at the Refectory of *Brother Bacon* (unavoidably postponed to the above day in consequence of the prolonged sojourn of the said Bacon in the land of *Ham*. At this Conclave, Robert Richard Scanlan, of Plymouth, and Hugh Barclay, of London, were proposed as Hap-hazard-out-of-door Blue Friars and Lay Brethren of the Order, and elected *nem. con.* Rosaries of Spanish beads were presented to the Brethren, and ordered to form part of the monastic paraphernalia of future conclaves. Under an especial dispensation from the Prior, one flagon of Champagne, and a runlet of Claret were added to the Refectory Stores." The papers read on this occasion were :—

The Prior: "Recollections of the Old Plymouth Theatre."

Locke: "Reginald and Rosalie; an Essay in Rhyme."

Bacon: "On Pushing in Life."

Roger: "A Lecture on Hats."

"1831: June 2nd. The Eighth Quarterly Conclave was held at the Refectory of Brother Roger, on which occasion a *Trifling* refectory contribution from the *Incip.* was added to the usual repast under a dispensation from the Prior, and the thanks of the Order voted to the said *Incip.* for her kind present. The following original papers were then read :

The Prior: "On Carving."

Locke: " A Leaf or two from the Volume of an Antiquary, published A.D. 2000."
Bacon: " On Vice Versâ."
Roger: " Knockers *v.* House Bells."

The next entry in the " Records " introduces us to another old and highly-respected Plymouthian, Mr. John Collier. The entry reads: " On July 11th, 1831, the Fraternity embarked in the barge of their Cellarman, John Collier, on a sea voyage, for the purpose of taking possession of and consecrating one of those amphibious samples of public property commonly called a Beach or Strand, in the immediate vicinity of the Shag Rock. A full description of this ceremony will be found among the papers of Brother Roger in the Blue Box.* On the completion of all the necessary duties of consecration, the said John Collier was proposed and unanimously elected a Lay Brother of the Order of Blue Friars, and on the following day his Patent of appointment, investing him with all Lay Privileges, was transmitted to him by the Prior. A letter of acknowledgment from Brother Collier is deposited among the Records in the Blue Box." This epistle is as follows :—

"Plymouth, 20th July, 1831.

Dear Sirs,

I have to apologise for having so long delayed to acknowledge the receipt of your very gratifying communication, stating that it had been pleased *nem. con.* to elect me a lay Brother of your venerable Order, accompanied with the patent of appointment duly signed and sealed. Allow me to express my warmest acknowledgments for this unexpected and distinguished honour, and to assure you that my humble abilities shall be exerted in promoting the laudable views of this highly-gifted Fraternity, by a faithful observance of all its laws and ordinances, and that it will at all times

---

* The length and personal character of this witty and interesting paper precludes our quoting here, but we shall endeavour to give a summary of it in the second part of our book, amongst the " Blue Friar Pleasantries."

afford me much pleasure when I have an opportunity of contributing in any wise to the enjoyment of its members.

I much regret that pressing business and absence in the country have prevented me sooner from assuring you that I have the honour to be, with due consideration,
   Gentlemen,
    Your very faithfull Servant and Brother,
        JNO. COLLIER.

To the Venerable Brothers Blue Friars."

Another interesting incident took place at the next meeting, October 21st, 1831, when Brother Roger presented to the Fraternity a Refectory Chaunt, composed for, and humbly dedicated to the Venerable Order of Blue Friars, by Alexander Dean Roche. The said chaunt was received most graciously, and ordered to be placed among the Records in the Blue Box, after which the said Alex. Dean Roche was unanimously elected a Lay Brother of the Order.* At this meeting, also, at the suggestion of Brother Bacon, enforced by certain rhythmical reasons to be found among his papers in the Blue Box, the following Toasts were ordered to be drank after Refection at every future Quarterly Conclave :—

 " God bless the Blue Friars." (hands joined)
 " Our Guardian Spirits—the Magpie and Owl."
 " The Mysteries of the Order."
 " The Lay Brethren."
 " The Lay Sisterhood."

The following invitation to attend a Conclave has been found amongst the papers, but we do not find that any such meeting was held on the date specified: it must therefore have fallen through :—

  " Sir Bacon : be it known to you,
  By order of our Prior Blue,

---

* The words of this chaunt will be given in the second part of the volume.

That, on the ninth of next December,
At Five o'clock P.M., remember!
The next high Conclave would be holden
(In coats of Blue, and buttons golden)
At Friar Locke's; and Bacon, mind ye,
To leave your *impudence* behind ye,
And bring a *more than usual* share
Of reverence, lest the Prior spare
' More kicks than halfpence.' 'There's the rub,'
And so, sir, *mind!*
                                    Your PRIOR-SUB.
Cell of Locke, 19th *Nov.*, 1831."

Passing over one or two meetings, we come to the Eleventh Quarterly Conclave, held September 20th, 1832, when it is recorded that "John Herrick Macaulay, the Prior of Repton, in Derbyshire, was elected and admitted by accumulation* to the dignity of Blue Cardinal, and took the oaths and his seat accordingly."

The invitation to Mr. Macaulay to join the Brotherhood was conveyed in the following formal document, a copy of which was found amongst the B.F. papers:—

"Tuck, Locke, Roger, Bacon, Founders of the jolliest of all jolly Orders of Friars, ycleped the Blue.

"To their lusty and well-beloved Cousin in the flesh, John Herrick Macaulay, sometime Master of the Ceremonies at Allmack's in the Western Hemisphere, but now Head-Gardener of the Parnassian Shrubbery at Repton in Derbyshire, send greeting.

"Forasmuch as it hath been made known unto us that thou the said John Herrick Macaulay have from time to time, and in sundry places, expressed in terms of commendable modesty an anxious desire to enter yourself a noviciate of the most enviable and envied Order of Blue Friars, to the end and intent that by deep study and patient and persevering adherence to the ascetic and

---

* Cumulative vote.

self-denying Canons of the said Order, thou mayest one day attain unto that apex of sublunary honors, a *Blue-Cardinal*;—And Whereas we have on manifold occasions, witnessed with much gratification thy mortifying but successful struggles at abstaining from indulging in the sins of the flesh (after dinner), and contenting thyself with thin potations from the vineyards of Chateau Margaux.—For these and other cogent reasons, best known to our Order, us hereunto moving—We do hereby summon the said J. H. M. to be and appear before us in proper person, at the cell of Brother Locke, *on Thursday next, at Five of the Clock in the Afternoon*, at a certain Conclave of the Order to be then and there holden. At which time and place thou wilt be required to answer such questions, assent to such ceremonies, and exhibit such proofs of good living, as the abovenamed Founders of this most glorious Order may in their infallible wisdom deem expedient to exact as testimonials of thy fitness for performing the duties of that exalted station to which thou dost aspire—and herein fail not at your peril.

Given at the Refectory of His Jolliness, Prior Tuck, this 17th day of September, 1832, and in the Fourth year of our Foundation."

At the next Conclave (November 9th, 1832), amongst other things noted, was the production of an original Paper by Brother Roger—" On Buttons : containing an account of the Installation of the Blue Cardinal."*

On November 29th, 1832, at a special morning Refection, it was resolved :—" That each Brother do make a fair copy of such original papers as he may have written for the Order, and consigned to the Blue Box, for the purpose of being bound together. Also, that half a ream of yellow paper be divided among the brethren—the

---

* See " Pleasantries."

copies to be made according to a design to be furnished by Brother Bacon. The original papers overhauled and a partial selection made and left for future consideration as to the propriety of publishing them under the title of ' Transactions of the Blue Friars.' "

On March 5th, 1833, Lay Brother Robert Scanlan, limner in Ordinary to the Fraternity, was allowed to be present under a general dispensation from the Order.

At this Conclave it was resolved :—" That at the next Conclave of the Order each of the Brethren instead of producing an Original Paper as heretofore, do revise, correct, alter and make a fair copy of one of his papers already deposited in the Blue Box, with a view to its being published hereafter among ' The Transactions of the Blue Friars.' That a copy of the said ' Transactions' when published be presented, handsomely bound, to Lay Brother Scanlan, with the kind regards of the Fraternity." And then follows this remarkable entry :—" That the Sacristan do purchase a sixteenth share of a Ticket in the Glasgow Lottery to be drawn on the 17th of the ensuing month, April ; the said Ticket to be entered in the name of the Blue Friars."

Brother Bacon presented a jar of Olives for the use of the Order; and in the course of the evening Brother Scanlan made a sketch of the Brethren seated round a table, as the foundation of a picture to be hereafter composed in honour of the Order. Where is the picture ?*

On October 30th, Mr. Thomas Edwin Gosling, of Plymouth, and Mr. William Money, of Hanover Street, Hanover Square, London, Surgeon, were proposed and elected Lay Brethren of the Order.

At the same meeting it was resolved :—" That each of

---

* Mr. Scanlan was an artist residing in Plymouth, about this time. An engraved portrait of Mr. Geo. Wightwick, by him, was published in the *Library of the Fine Arts*, 1832.

the Brethren do now pay into the hands of the Sacristan the sum of Five Shillings, to meet the current expenses of the Order.

"Also that the Prior and Sub-Prior do forthwith get prepared a Snuff-box with the emblems of the Order emblazoned thereon, and transmit the same to His Portliness the Blue Cardinal, with the kindest mems. from the Fraternity."

Brother Roger presented each of his Blue Brethren with an emblematical Ring, which was ordered henceforth to form part of the Monastic paraphernalia. We regret that we have not succeeded in obtaining a specimen of the B.F. Snuff-box, but, as two of the rings have been placed in our hands, we have engraved one of them for the benefit of our readers.

The next event is perhaps the most interesting and noteworthy of any to be found in the Records of the Order. It stands thus:—

"1833 : November 23rd. It having been determined by the Fraternity to avail themselves of the visit to this neighbourhood of the great Hogarthian spirit of the age, Charles Mathews, to confer on him the dignity of a Blue Friar, together with a full participation in all the privileges and advantages appertaining thereto :—

"A special Open Conclave of the Order was holden this day, at the Refectory of Brother Bacon, for the above purpose. On which occasion Lay Brother Scanlan, together with John Franklin and Henry Giles, partook with the Fraternity of a *Siamesed* Feast of Mirth and Mutton, and an overflow of Wit and Wine. His Jolliness Prior Tuck, in an appropriate address, informed the Brother Elect of the dignity about to be conferred on him. He then explained to him the constitution and objects of

Brother Prism (Mr. Charles Mathews).

the Venerable Order and presented him with his Monastic Diploma, together with a Snuff-box illuminated with the emblems of the Order. The various privileges to which he was thereby admitted were announced to him by the Sub-Prior, Brother Locke, and the Health of Friar Prism drank with long and repeated acclamations. The pithy eloquence of his reply was only exceeded by the earnest humility of his acknowledgments on receiving so unexpected and invaluable a distinction. The evening was spent by the Brethren in a continuous stream of intellectual luxury."

To this there is appended the declaration of the newly elected Brother with the autograph as follows:—

"1833: November 23.

I, Brother Prism, of the Venerable Order of Blue Friars, having this day received my Diploma, investing me with all the privileges appertaining to this Fraternity, and exempting me from the performance of such Monastic duties as my constant and unavoidable absence from the Conclaves would render 'extremely inconvenient,' do hereby pledge myself, so far as in my power lies, to maintain and uphold the dignity, jollity, and good fellowship of the Order, whenever an opportunity for so doing shall present itself.

By the Hand of a Blue Friar,

(Signed) PRISM."

The following is the text of the Address to Friar

Prism before his election as a Brother of the Order :—

"Sir,

The object of the Order of Blue Friars, who have now the pleasure of seeing you at their Refectory, is to cultivate social intercourse between persons duly appreciating the philosophy of humour and wit, as well as to pursue subjects of dramatic and other literature in which the intellect or imagination are found occasionally to display themselves under more sober forms. To the accomplishment of this end quarterly Conclaves are specially holden, at which it is imperative on the Brethren to produce a certain number of essays or papers connected with the subjects alluded to, and which are finally deposited in the Archives of the Society, with a view to ultimate publication.

The Order consists at present of five Brethren only—the four Founders, viz., Tuck (the Prior), Locke (the Sub-Prior), Friars Bacon and Roger (the latter being Clerk and Sacristan), and a Cardinal in the person of Sir John Heyrick Macaulay, Prior of Repton in Derbyshire. There are a few Lay Brothers, who occasionally visit the Refectory, but who are not required to uphold the Archives of the Order.

The Order are possessed of a set of chimes, and an appropriate costume—of the latter little need be said; but of the former (viz., the chimes) it may perhaps be pertinent to remark, that, differing from chimes in general, there is only *one* bell, which, in form, if not in all respects resembling, is scarcely distinguishable from a wine glass, and tho' but one, it possesses sundry clappers which will be found on all occasions to discourse most excellent music:

Chime, Cerulean Brothers, chime,
Loud your peal, and true your time.

Moreover, there is an appropriate seal and motto belonging to the Order, whose characteristic emblems are an owl and a magpie, the first denoting wit, the latter betokening discretion.

The Fraternity, Sir, perceiving in you every quality and qualification calculated to shed lustre upon their Order; observing, in truth, in your person an accomplished specimen of all the varied excellencies that go to the constitution of a Blue Friar, do elect you into their Fraternity under the distinguished appellation of Friar Prism, but without imposing upon you the obligation of contributing to their literary treasures further than your arduous duties elsewhere shall permit, and your inclination impel.

I, therefore, the Prior of the Fraternity, on my own behalf and in the name of Friars Locke, Bacon, and Roger, do present you with this diploma as an evidence of your claim to the full participation in all the advantages of the Brotherhood—a distinction (not to vaunt ourselves) for which Princes and Potentates have sighed for and sighed in vain.

* You will have the full benefit of Clergy as it regards the spiritual and bodily cheer that will be yours whenever you visit the Prior, Sir John of Repton, our trusty and well-beloved Cardinal. You will have the right of gratuitously claiming all the "Love, Law, and Physic" that can be afforded from our store of brotherly attachment, and by our legal and medical professors Friars Tuck and Bacon. You will have free access to the records, deeds, and original papers of the fraternity by due application to the Sacristan, Brother Roger. You will have at command whatever Masonic skill, I, as your Sub-Prior Locke—an architect, and no Freemason—can furnish; and lastly, you will have the privilege of contributing to the moral, philosophical, and mirthful stores of the Society; by which you will acquire an ever-increasing advantage to yourself—yourself, sir, individually—your situation as a donor in this peculiar instance being similar to that of the delectable Juliet, whose words are no doubt familiar to your ears:—

'The more I give—the more I *have*.'

Such, sir, are the advantages you enjoy in becoming a Blue Brother."

A very interesting account of the installation of Mr. Mathews as a "Brother Blue" is given in an article published in *Fraser's Magazine* for March, 1836, entitled "My acquaintance with the late Charles Mathews," the author being Brother Locke (Mr. George Wightwick). This article will be found reprinted in full in this collection, and we therefore do not think it necessary to give any extracts from it in this place.

Nothing worthy of note occurred until April 29th, 1834, when we find it recorded that—" At this Conclave the *ornithological emblems* of the Order, *in proprias personis*,

---

* There appear to have been two addresses, the latter portion having apparently been prepared and delivered by Locke, the former by the Prior Tuck.—ED.

were introduced and presented to the Fraternity by the Sacristan, Brother Roger. They were received with reverential honours, duly consecrated and ordered to form part of the Refectory paraphernalia at all future Conclaves."

The next matter of interest recorded was on the 8th August, 1834, when "During the sitting of the Conclave, Sir Thomas Dyke Acland, Bart., and his son were announced, and by general consent admitted. The stay of the former with the Fraternity, tho' short, was of sufficient duration to convince them of his possessing all the requisites of a 'Reg'lar Blue, and no mistake.'"

The Fraternity at this time appear to have been more free in their admission of outsiders, and did not restrict their Conclaves to the fully qualified Blue Brothers, for we find on December 12th of the same year the following Resolutions proposed and carried, *nem. con.*:—

"Resolved: That at any of the future Conclaves of the Order it shall be competent for each of the Brethren at whose Refectory such Conclave for the time being shall be holden, to invite one or more of the Lay Brethren of the Order to be then and there present. Provided always that such invitation be given with the consent and under the signatures of each of the other Brethren." Also the following stringent rule as to the original papers:—

"That in future no paper which is produced and read by any of the Brethren at any of the Grand Conclaves shall be received as 'Original,' unless it be warranted by such Brother to have been written by him expressly for such Conclave, and has not been previously read before any other society. Any Brother offending herein to be liable to the penalties imposed by Canon 5 of this Order."

A curious entry follows the above which shows how

closely business and play were allied in the minds of the Brethren :—

" That an alteration be made in the Costumes to be worn at the future Conclaves of the Order, viz., the abduction of monastic noses, and the induction of Blue Surplices and Cowls, &c."

The Sacristan was also instructed to order one gross of B.F. vest buttons for the use of the Order, an illustration of which is here shown.

On December 27th, 1834, the Brethren met in Cœnal Conclave at the Refectory of His Jolliness Prior Tuck, for the purpose of displaying their belligerent powers on a detachment of Metropolitan Oysters, sent to them by Lay Brother Argent, and after a smart skirmish fully succeeded in astonishing the "natives." At this meeting Mr. William Eastlake was admitted as a Lay Brother.

A rhythmical invitation was issued to the Brethren on this occasion, of which the following is a copy :—

"A SONG :
(Over true.)
Boys of Blue Coats and of Cowl,
Boys of Magpie and of Owl,
Hearken! 'tis your Prior speaks :
Cock your ears, and ope your beaks!

Oysters, far from Plymouth fed,
Nurtur'd in famed Melton's bed,
Fed in London's choicest shops,
Seek to greet your longing chops.

Oysters upwrenched from the deep
When once landed will not keep ;
At thy Prior's call resort, or
Their time of keeping will be shorter.

Deep within thy Prior's cell,
As tolls of one o'clock the bell,
Will the pearly tribe be spread
With ale and pepper, salt and bread.

> At one o'clock (d'ye hear me say ?)
> At one o'clock this very day,
> Or the close-lipp'd fools will be
> Spoilt for your maws, as you may see.
>
> Come, then, and partake this lunch
> Aided by whisky, ale, or punch;
> Be punctual, or my stomach tells
> You'll nothing have, beside the shells!
>
> *Grand Chorus—*
> Whisky, frisky, galleinaneous, high jinks, heigh-ho !
> Oyterundem, flibberty-gibbety, dideroo, whack !

1834: *Dec.* 24."

The Surplices and Cowls mentioned in a previous note were first used at the Meeting held on January 20th, 1835.

The next entry is of a sorrowful character, the first of a series which we shall have occasion to allude to later on.

"May 18th, 1835. Poor Brother Prism arrived at the residence of John Franklin, Esq., in the Royal Victualling Yard, Plymouth, in a state of irrecoverable illness. From whence he was removed to No. 12, Lockyer Street, Plymouth, on the 12th of June following, in which house he died on the 28th day of the same month, in the 59th year of his age, and anniversary of his birth.

Requiescat in pace."

We would again refer our readers to the paper by Mr. Wightwick, " My acquaintance with the late Charles Mathews," for some interesting particulars relative to the last hours and death of this famed Comedian, who was buried in St. Andrew's Church, Plymouth, a handsome monument being erected to his memory with the following inscription, the eulogium being from the pen of his friend George Wightwick :—

"Near this Spot are deposited the honoured Remains of Charles Mathews, Comedian, Born 28th June, 1776, Died 28th June, 1835. Not to commemorate that Genius which his Country acknowledged and rewarded, and Men of every Nation confessed; nor to record the worth which secured the respect and attachment of his admirers and friends; but as an humble Tribute to his devoted, unvarying affection and indulgence as a Husband and Father, this Tablet is erected in sorrowing Love and grateful Remembrance by his bereaved Wife and Son.

BY A FRIEND.
All England mourn'd, when her Comedian died,
A public loss that ne'er might be supplied;
For who could hope such varied gifts to find,
All rare and exquisite, in one combined?
The private virtues that adorn'd his breast,
Crowds of admiring Friends with tears confess'd:
Only to Thee, O God! the grief was known
Of those who rear this Monumental Stone;
The Son and Widow, who, with Bosoms torn,
The best of Fathers and of Husbands mourn,
Of all this public, social, private woe,
Here lies the cause—Charles Mathews sleeps below."

At the next Quarterly Conclave of the Blue Friars (September 23rd, 1835), it is recorded that Henry Gyles and Lay Brother Edwin Lovell were present by invitation, the former of whom, after passing a severe and splendid examination, was admitted by acclamation as a full Brother of this venerable order, under the Monastic title of *Brother Somno*.

Lay Brother Edwin was at the same time promoted by unanimous consent to the dignity of a full Brother of this venerable order under the Monastic title of *Brother Glastonbury*, who this day enriched the Refectory department by the munificent donation of a superb silver-edged Claret Ewer, which was immediately consecrated, and ordered to be used at all future Conclaves of the Order. Then follows the declarations of the newly-elected Brothers, with their Monastic signatures.

In the "Book of the Records" the signed declaration of *Brother Somno* (Mr. Henry Gyles) was hidden by a sheet of paper being wafered over it, and his name and the titles of the papers read by him at several subsequent meetings obliterated in a most systematic manner. The reason for this action is not explained, but on the 8th of November, 1837, we find this entry. "The resignation of Somno as a Brother of the Order of Blue Friars, was this day received and accepted. All the papers relating to this painful subject will be found in the Blue Box, in a parcel indorsed 'Somno's resignation and discharge.'" The latter word is emphasized by being placed within inverted commas.

That there was some disagreement is evident, though the nature of the trouble does not appear. Mr. Henry Gyles was a gentleman residing in Lockyer Street, Plymouth, and he is specially mentioned in the paper on Charles Mathews as being his most intimate friend and host and as having conducted the funeral arrangements of the great Comedian.

The following letter found amongst the papers in the Blue Box must be accepted as the only explanation we can offer for the secession of Brother Somno :—

"Dear Jacobson,

As some of the principal features which attracted my regard towards the Blue Friars have changed countenance, and as the mode of publishing their compositions is not in accordance with my notions of liberal fellowship, I beg leave to withdraw my name from the Club and am, dear Jacobson,

Yours most sincerely,
HENRY GYLES.

Windsor Terrace, *8th Nov.*, 1837."

Returning after this brief digression, we find that the next Meeting was held on the 12th April, 1836, when amongst other matters of interest it is recorded that "His Jolliness the Prior presented to the Fraternity a beautifully engraved likeness of our revered Brother Prism, which was ordered to be framed and produced at all future Conclaves of the Order. Brother Locke also deposited in the Blue Box the M.S. of his paper, entitled 'My acquaintance with Mathews,' published in *Fraser's Magazine*, and previously mentioned. Another addition to the Refectory paraphernalia was also made by the presentation of five antique wine-glasses by Brother Roger."

At the following Meeting, May 12th, 1836, an important decision was arrived at, viz., "That the recent additions to the Monastic Costume—the Surplices, Cowls, &c.—should only be indued on such extraordinary occasions as may be determined on from time to time hereafter, and that at future Conclaves the Brethren shall appear in the dress originally agreed upon and duly set forth in Canon 4." It is difficult to understand why these changes were made, except that some of the number did not approve of innovations, and preferred to act according to the original scheme, as set forth by the founders.

The Sacristan was ordered to procure half a gross of B.F. Buttons for the use of the Order, from which it is evident that the Brethren frequently required new garments, either incidental to a change of costume, or to the shedding of those necessary and useful appendages induced by unwonted hilarity and good living combined. Brother Bacon also presented the Fraternity with what are called "Barcelona Rosaries," which we should judge were rosaries made by stringing together a number of the nuts which take their name from this celebrated Spanish town.

An important entry occurs on the next date recorded:—
"That each of the Brethren do correct or rewrite one of the papers he has already contributed to the Blue Box,

in order to its being offered for publication ; viz. :—
  The Prior: ' A Merry Christmas.'
  Locke: ' A Dinner Party.'
  Bacon: ' Architectural Physics.'
  Roger: ' On Laughing.'
  Somno: ' An Essay on Digitology.' "

This was the beginning of a movement which resulted in the publication of the "Blue Friar Pleasantries" in *Fraser's Magazine*, as mentioned in an early part of this work, although these contributions did not reach the dignity and magnitude aspired to by the brethren of the Order, as set forth in the entries immediately following.

It was proposed by Brother Locke, and adopted, that the foregoing, and such other papers as may be determined on hereafter, be sent to Messrs. Ridgway, of London, Booksellers, in order that the necessary arrangements may be made as soon as possible for their being published by him in one or more volumes under the title of "Blue Friar Pleasantries," to which end the said Brother Locke produced and read an "Introductory Paper," mercifully tending to disperse some of the mists which would otherwise becloud the comprehensions of the uninitiated during the perusal of the said "Pleasantries."* At this same meeting "The Prior read a Precept he had that morning received from his Portliness, John Herricke, the Blue Cardinal, dated from his Priory at Repton, enjoining the Brethren to meet him in Conclave, at the Royal Hostelrie, in Plymouth, on the 31st day of December next, at six of the clock at eve, to which precept the Prior ordered strict obedience.

Here followeth the Cardinal's Precept:

Wete ye well y^t the nechst Conclavus off the Venerabil Order of Blew Friars is yntended to bee holdyne

---

* This Paper appears on pages 4—9 of this work.

at the Celle of youre Cardinale, inne the Royal Hostelrie, Plym^{th.} the 31st daie off the moneth off December neckst, at the stryckenne houre of sixxe off the clocke at eve. Wherfor we wylle and doe strecklie charge and consayle you y^t ye then and there doe appeyne, and doe ayde and helpe in eche soche affaynes and proceedynges which from tyme immymorryall have been socht and askitt at the handdes off trew Blew Friars for the spede and gode off the Orderne on lyke convenance, or whyche may then and there be demaunded off you.

Written at oure Priorrie in Reppington, the 23rd daie of the Moneth off October, MDCCCXXXVI.

John,   [seal]
(By permission)
Cardinale.

☞ *Tuck (Prior) is strecklie enjoyned to issue these precepts to Broderres Locke, Bacon, Roger."*

Another interesting matter is recorded here, viz., that "A venerable relic from the extinct monastery of the White Friars, in Plymouth, was presented to the Fraternity, and ordered to be kept as a Memento Mori."

During this Conclave, "Brother Roger introduced to the Fraternity an incipient Candidate for future honours of Blue Friarhood, who received the blessings of the Prior and the Brethren; and it is hoped he may live to be in due time admitted as one of the Order under the title of *Brother Optimus*." Who Brother Optimus was is gathered from the following loose memorandum found amongst the Records, which gives some other interesting information :—

"The contents of this 'Blue Box,' as well as those of another smaller one, marked 'B.F,' together with the 'Glastonbury Claret

Jug,' and all other Blue Friar Relics, of whatsoever kind, which may be found extant after the respective deaths of Brothers Locke and Roger, become the sole property of John Best Newton, who was duly admitted as a member of the Venerable Order of Blue Friars, at the Conclave held at the Refectory of Brother Roger, on the 25th day of October, 1836, by the Title of '*Brother Optimus*,' and which will be found recorded in the 'Blue Book' among the proceedings of the said Conclave."*

Next follows an important item relative to the "Blue Friar Pleasantries." On March 7th, 1837, it was reported by Brother Locke, that in accordance with the Resolution passed at the last Conclave respecting the publication of the "Blue Friar Pleasantries," he had communicated with Messrs. Ridgway thereon; that in consequence of those gentlemen having ceased to publish works of fiction they were under the necessity of declining the offer of the Brethren, but strongly recommended their papers being brought out separately in *Fraser's Magazine.* That on a sample of the "Pleasantries" being submitted for Mr. Fraser's consideration, he had rapturously accepted the offices of Printer and Publisher, and "Monthly Nurse" to the literary bantlings of the Venerable Order; and with a flattering eulogium on those then under his protection, "intimated his intention of adopting the same, and such others of like quality as may be sent to him, at the rate of Ten Guineas per sheet, to be paid to the respective authors thereof." Of course these terms were accepted.

The following is a complete list of "Blue Friar Pleasantries" which appeared in *Fraser* from 1837 to 1840 inclusive, from which it will be seen that Brother Locke (Mr. Wightwick) was the chief contributor:—

1837.
  1. Introductory ... ... *Locke.*
  2. A Scene in Ticklebrook Church.

---

* John Best Newton (Brother Optimus) was introduced as a child in his mother's arms. *Vide* letter dated June 10th, 1889.

List of "Pleasantries."

3.	Play-going Days	*Locke.*
4.	A Few Hints for the Promulgation of a New Science	*Somno.*
5.	Christmas	*Tuck.*
6.	My First Party	*Roger.*
7.	Lubin's Log	*Locke.*
8.	Modern Times	*Tuck.*
9.	A Dinner Party	*Locke.*
10.	Some Account of the Natural and Artificial History of Corks	,,
11.	Little Boney. A School Reminiscence	,,
12.	Travelling all Night	,,
13.	Priestby. A Fragment, after the fashion of the celebrated Poem "Rokeby"	,,
14.	The Bridal	,,
15.	The Amusing Fellow	,,
16.	Report of a Visit to the Consolidated National Knowledge Company	,,

1838.

17.	Introductory	*Roger.*
18.	Origin of Mulligatawny Soup	*Tuck.*
19.	Gravy Soup	*Locke.*
20.	Ox Tail Soup	*Roger.*
21.	Pea Soup	*Bacon.*
22.	The Man of Few Words	*Locke.*
23.	A Midsummer Eve's Dream	,,
24.	Reflections at an Evening Party	,,
25.	The Theatrical Man-iac	,,
26.	The Assembly	,,
27.	Mutton Sonnets	,,

1839.

28.	Rather Grave for a Pleasantry	*Locke.*
29.	Neglected Poetry	*Tuck.*
30.	Holyday Folks	*Locke.*
31.	Locke in London	,,

32.	Selections from the B.F. Orchestra ...	*Locke.*
33.	Plymouth Hoe ⎫ Breakwater ⎬ Eddystone Lighthouse ⎭	,,
34.	A School Meeting ...	,,

1840.

35.	Popping the Question according to Modern Experience	,,
36.	Popping the Question according to Shakspeare	,,
37.	A Guinea Fling, being a Letter from Locke in London to his Blue Brethren in the Country; dated Jany., 1840	,,

The only event worthy of mention which occurred in the year 1837, was that on the 26th of August " The Blue Friars' Sauce," with appropriate label by Brother Roger, was introduced, and ordered to form a Refectory item at all future Conclaves of the Order. This justly celebrated sauce was exceedingly popular among gastronomic epicures for many years. The original label, which we reproduce on the opposite page, bears the seal with the emblems of the Order and some exceedingly witty lines.

More than twelve months elapsed before another Conclave of the Order was held, the twenty-eighth quarterly meeting taking place on the 19th September, 1838, when nothing of especial interest transpired.

After this, a further period of nearly eighteen months elapsed without a meeting, for reasons which do not transpire. But we find that on the 17th March, 1840, the twenty-ninth Conclave was held, at which this matter was fully considered, and it was resolved " That in order to avoid the recurrence of so unprecedented and unpardonable a hiatus between the meetings of the

"Locke not dressed according to the rules of the Order—one bottle of port wine."

"Bacon: dinner not on table till ten minutes before six—one bottle of Vidonia."

"The Prior fines himself for his culpable lenity to the above offenders just what seemeth good to him, and is sure to be so to the rest of the Order."

Another entry runs thus:—"His Jolliness the Prior fined one dozen of *Friar's Balsam* for not producing any original paper at the Conclave held on the above day (March 5th, 1841)."

Two other notes must be made, in passing, of incidents which took place at the Twenty-ninth Grand Conclave: one being the delivery of a paper by Brother Roger, entitled "A Chronological Retrospect of Blue Friarism: Part I.";* and the other that "New Caps and Proboscee were indued." Barclay Fox was present on this occasion under a special dispensation from the Prior.

At the Thirtieth Grand Conclave, held on April 21st, 1840, several matters of interest are recorded.

Brother Glastonbury was present by proxy, in the shape of a gorgeous Turbot, evidently from the coast of *Fin*land, and was duly received by the brethren; after which flagons of Bilge, Pump, Ditch, and Spring water were placed on the board, but on being sparingly tasted by the brethren, despite the persuasive eulogy and example of His Jolliness the Prior, it was considered best at all times "to let WELL alone."

An adjournment to the post-prandial Refectory, however, disclosed a feast which had evidently been prepared under the rival superintendence of Bacchus and Pomona —whose choicest productions the brethren discussed

---

* As this paper contains a most interesting *resumé* of the whole proceedings of the Order, and throws light on some obscure portions of the Records, we propose to print it *in extenso* in this volume.

with laudable impartiality. It has been noted elsewhere that ladies were, as a rule, precluded from attending these solemn meetings, but on this occasion it is recorded that "in the course of the evening the Prioress and certain Lay Sisters perambulated the Refectory in orthodox procession, and were entertained by the Brethren after the manner of Blue Friars towards their sisterhood."

The thirty-first Grand Conclave, held on the 21st July, was shorn of the presence of Brother Bacon, this being the first meeting held since the foundation of the Order without the full attendance of its original members. A local incident of some interest furnished a theme for Brother Locke, who contributed a poetical lament for St. Andrew's Bell, deceased. This, we presume, was at the time the great tenor bell in St. Andrew's tower became cracked and had to be re-cast.

ST. ANDREW'S BELL.

It is the year of Christian grace
  Seventeen hundred fifty-nine:
The furnace yields its molten wealth
  Drawn from the subterranean mine.

The mould is teeming with its birth,
  The *Bel*-dam mutters many a spell;
Freed from the womb—lo! stands reveal'd
  St. Andrew's silent tenor bell.

And now its iron tongue depends,
  (What varied tales that tongue shall tell!
No longer silent, hark! it speaks:—
  St. Andrew's sounding tenor bell!

Behold the scaffoldage, the ropes,
  The force mechanic—sinew power;
It mounts! St. Andrew speed it well!
  It swings within St. Andrew's tower.

Hark to the joyous peal aloft:
  What gladsome notes our hearts elate.
The mighty octave clamours loud,
  One, two, three, four, five, six, seven, eight!

Fraternity, as the Records of the Order have this day presented, the Grand Conclaves shall in future be held in strict conformity with the 4th Canon of the Order, viz., on the 20th day of the months of January, April, July, and October, respectively."

Reproduction of Sauce Label :—

THE BLUE FRIARS' SAUCE.

Of various Compounds used t' excite the *fauces*,
𝔅𝔩𝔲𝔢 𝔉𝔯𝔦𝔞𝔯𝔰' 𝔖𝔞𝔲𝔠𝔢 transcends all other sauces ;
To weak digestions 'tis an analeptic,
A panacæa for most ills dyspeptic :
This piquant zest, with butter mix'd or gravy,
Hath sav'd the Brethren many a sad "*peccavi ;*"
And render'd FISH, from Turbot to Red Mullet,
As easy of digestion as Boil'd Pullet.
RUMP STEAKS, CHOPS, GAME, COLD MEAT—*id omne genus*,
Are dead without it, as Canova's Venus ;
But *with* it—trust one GRAY and four 𝔅𝔩𝔲𝔢 𝔉𝔯𝔦𝔞𝔯𝔰—
" *E'en in our* HASHES *live their wonted fires !*"

TO BE PROCURED ONLY AT
NORTHCROFT'S, (late HOLMAN,)
CHEMIST,—PLYMOUTH.
*Where every other Fish Sauce may be obtained.**

---

* We believe this justly-celebrated Sauce is still to be obtained in Plymouth at the establishment of Mr. Allen, George-street, the successor of those whose names appear on the label here given.—ED.

It was also decided " That the Prior do procure a new edition of the minor seal of the Order, for the especial use of His Jolliness—and the Sacristan a Monastic Snuff-Box, duly emblazoned, to be sent to His Portliness the Blue Cardinal" (Macaulay). Snuff-taking was much in vogue in those days, and we find it also recorded that Brother Locke presented his own Monastic Snuff-box for the general use of the Order, which was thankfully received. In fact the snuff-box was a prominent and indispensable part of the paraphernalia of the Order, and is especially mentioned in the Canons provided for its governance. It may be further mentioned that a special snuff was manufactured by Messrs. Fribourg and Freyer, London, under the name " Blue Friars' Mixture," and that it is still supplied by that well-known firm of the Haymarket.

Another item recorded on the same date has reference to the Refectory arrangements, and is worthy of mention :—

" That, inasmuch as by the Rules of the Order the Fraternity are limited to one dish of fruit only for their post-prandial amusement—each Brother at whose Refectory a Grand Quarterly Conclave shall be holden, is enjoined to produce *a goodly-sized dish* filled and piled up with an ample supply of such fruits as may then be in season or can be procured—any Brother failing in this injunction to be at the mercy of the Prior, in the imposition of such penalty as His Jolliness shall see fit to inflict."

What those penalties were may be gathered from a few entries at the end of the volume of " Records," from which it appears that the Brethren rarely failed in their duty in these important matters. Among the entries of " Fines " are the following :—

" Roger not dressed according to the rules of the Order—one quart bottle of port wine."

Although fierce tumult frights the land,
  The loyal chime their anthem ring;
One, two, three, four, five, six, seven, eight !
  God save the second George our King !

Lo ! now the *seven* are silent all,
  Death hovers o'er with shadowy wing :
The tenor bell alone exclaims,
  Pray for the soul of George the King !

Again the eight ring forth their joy :
  Another George is crown'd to-day !
Again the tenor sounds alone,
  That all for our third George may pray.

For George—our fourth—'tis sounding now,
  And now it rings *his* funeral knell.
Now for a princess' wedding swings ;
  Now tolls—she's dead, we lov'd so well.

Again, as woe had never been,
  The peal for our fourth William ring :
Again the tenor sadly tells,
  He's gone !—the good old Sailor-King !

And yet—another peal—the last :
  A Queen is crown'd and wedded well :
It will *not* toll Victoria's death,—
  'Tis gone ! that good old tenor bell.

No more in wedding joy, the twain
  Shall hear it take its gladsome part ;
No more shall love-'reft widow feel
  Its tones strike sadly on her heart.

'Tis voiceless now. An envious rent
  For aye its sounding might doth quell ;
Another now hath ta'en its place,—
  'Tis gone—that good old tenor bell !

              Locke, B. F.

    The full complement of members attended the next Conclave, at which nothing of special interest transpired, if we except the admission of sundry Misses McCullum as Lay Sisters of the Order.

    The next entry is of more than ordinary significance,

and must be given in full:—" December 18th, 1840. This day is one of mournful recollection for the Fraternity, as it closed the earthly career of our sincerely valued and truly valuable friend and Brother, *John Herricke Macaulay*, the Cardinal of our Order; who, after lingering three days from an attack of Paralysis, was released from all the cares of this world, at his residence, the Priory of Repton, in Derbyshire. Much beloved as he was by his relatives, and warmly as he was esteemed by an unusually extensive circle of friends and acquaintance, there are few to whom the full estimate of his intrinsic worth is more accurately known, or who will more deeply deplore the loss of such a man, than his Brethren of the Order of Blue Friars. He was elected Cardinal of the Order on the 20th day of September, 1832."

It may be remembered that Mr. Macaulay was at one time Head Master of the New Grammar School, Plymouth, and there may be some amongst us now who have cause to remember his strict discipline with his pupils.

There is a tablet to his memory in St. Andrew's Church with the following inscription :—

"Sacred to the Memory of the Revd. John Heyrick Macaulay, M.A., of Trinity College, Cambridge, late Head Master of Repton School, and formerly of the New Grammar School, Plymouth. By his accurate Scholarship, strict and impartial Discipline and unwearied Diligence, He enabled many of his pupils to attain Academic distinction. By his domestic Virtues, generous Hospitality, and high companionable qualities, He secured the devoted affection of his Family, and endeared himself to a large circle of acquaintance. To the Poor, he was a kind and liberal Benefactor: and the Regard entertained for his character, as a Christian Minister, is Recorded, where it was best known, on a worthier Monument at Repton, where he suddenly died, December 18, 1840, aged 42 years. As a tribute to his moral, social, and intellectual worth, This Tablet has been erected by his Friends and Pupils of this Neighbourhood."

The next entry of interest, dated March 5th, 1841,

explains more fully the imposition of a Fine on the Prior, to which we called attention just now, for amongst the list of papers entered as read, the Prior is set down as " Nil," and in a foot-note we are informed that " His Jolliness the Prior, having appeared at this Conclave without producing any original paper of his own composition, rendered himself amenable to the penalties in that case made and provided by Canon 5 of this venerable Order, whereby his cellar stands mulctable of one dozen of Friars' Balsam. This is the first violation of the above Canon since the foundation of the Order." This shows how well these worthy men followed the laws of their own creation, and how closely and lovingly they carried out the duties (self-imposed) which fell to them.

At a previous Conclave the Prior escaped this fine by the contribution of a short paper entitled " A Piteous Excuse," which we here present to our readers as a token of the friendly relations between the Brethren :—

"A Piteous Excuse.

Know ye, gentle and beloved Friars, that your Prior is suffering in mind, body, and estate. That the first is grievously affected by several very afflictive demands upon it, the second is sinking beneath the keenness of its ethereal inmate, and the last, within your Prior's remembrance, has never been in good repair, and of late years has become most grievously dilapidated. Your Prior is aware that in stating this account of himself he is more deeply interesting your benevolent hearts than by producing any paper on a subject in which he stands not prominently, and he anticipates that each loved Brother vie with his fellow in commending the present as one of your Prior's most laudable productions, inasmuch as it touches on a subject naturally the nearest and dearest to the heart of each—his welfare—and affords the opportunity of their bestowing upon him the tenderest sympathy, the most active exertion, and the most liberal assistance. 21st July, 1840."

A somewhat mysterious entry follows, under date May 6th, 1842, when it is recorded " That at this Conclave two *lay* Brethren were present of some strange order unknown to the Fraternity—but from their determined and cautious silence, coupled with the unequivocal slyness of their looks, they doubtless belonged to the Monastery of *La Trappe !*" Query, what were they ?

At the next meeting, May 9th, 1843 (again a gap of twelve months, it will be observed), William Robert Hicks, of Bodmin, a chance visitor to Brother Locke, was permitted to be present under a dispensation from His Jolliness the Prior. The name of Mr. Hicks is doubtless familiar to many of our readers, from a most interesting pamphlet recently published by Mr. W. F. Collier, which contains many amusing anecdotes, some of which, as specially appertaining to the Blue Friars, we hope to incorporate in the present volume.

On August 30th, 1843, an event of considerable interest took place, which was made the occasion of a display of loyalty on the part of the Blue Friars. "At five o'clock p.m., Her Most Gracious Majesty Queen Victoria, with her Royal Consort, Prince Albert, frighted our Monastery from its propriety by her arrival in Plymouth Sound in her steam yacht *Victoria and Albert*, under a Royal Salute from every Battery and *H*attery within her sacred ken. Such of the Brethren as were at their refections forsook their food and fled with most unwonted haste to greet the Royal Visitors. His Jolliness the Prior, with Brother Bacon, well-nigh became martyrs to a plethora of loyalty and beef in their zealous race to reach the Hoe on this ever-memorable occasion. On the following day Her Majesty and Royal Consort returned the monastic compliments by bowing their marked acknowledgments

as they passed the cells of Brothers Bacon and Roger. '*Vivant Victoria Regina et Albertus Princeps.*'"*

An interesting innovation was introduced at the next Quarterly Conclave, holden at the Refectory of Brother Bacon. This was, " That in future, each Brother at whose cell any Grand Conclave of the Order shall be holden do furnish for the edification of the Fraternity a list of the Refectorial items to be then and there forthcoming; to the end that each of the Brethren may take heed how far he may safely indulge his piscatorial or carnal appetite." This is one reason for the introduction of the now well-known *menu*-cards, an almost necessary adjunct of every feast, whether public or private.

Another enigma which we find it impossible to solve is propounded in the next entry: " The Magpie-ism at this Conclave derived a casual impetus from the unexpected presence of two gigantic *Black-guards*, the profuse looseness of whose costume only prevented their passing for a brace of indubitable *Tight-'uns* (Titans).

The only matter worthy of mention at the next two or three meetings, was that illuminated cards, with emblematical mottoes, were dispensed to each of the Brethren, whereon were emblazoned the principal Refectorial items to be then and there forthcoming. Wherefore His Jolliness (the Prior, at whose Refectory the Conclave was held) was much commended.

As it may be of interest to our readers to compare one of these illuminated menu-cards with some of those beautiful works of art so often seen in these days at civic and other banquets; we give as a separate plate a fac-simile of one of these productions from the stores of

---

* This visit is not mentioned by the Queen in " Leaves from the Journal of our Life in the Highlands," which gives particulars of several subsequent yachting tours.

the Blue Box referred to in a later paragraph. It must be noted, however, that the Blue Friars' menu cards were simply drawn in pen and ink, and though very ingenious they bear no comparison with their modern prototypes; this branch of industry having undergone a vast improvement during the last fifty years.

At the next meeting (October 10th, 1844), among the papers read was one by Brother Locke (Mr. Wightwick) on the " Plan and Specifications for the construction of a " Blue Friars' Lodge," a visionary scheme which was evidently like a " castle in the clouds."

We would it were possible to include in this work Mr. Wightwick's paper in its entirety, as descriptive of the drawing, a fac-simile of which forms the frontispiece to the present volume. The full title is as follows :—

" SPECIFICATION and Particular of sundry works of devilry to be done, in the construction of a *Blue Lodge* for the Blue Brethren, agreeable to the Plans hereto annexed, prepared by Brother Locke." Mr. Wightwick was well known in his profession as an authority in the matter of specifications, and we are informed that he was the author of a model specification adopted by the Society of Architects, which has served as a guide to the members of that fraternity through several successive generations. However that may be, certain it is that the document abounds in clever fancies, admirably adapted to its purpose; but we refrain from quoting it *in extenso*, fearing that some of our readers would fail to comprehend the technicalities used, and others might stigmatize it as too decidedly *blue* for publication.

The Refectorial arrangements at this Conclave were reported to be of " unsurpassable excellence both in quality and quantity, as the cards preserved in the Blue Box will amply testify. The virtues of a quatrain of champagne flasks were unfolded to the Brethren by four

Cerulean Nuns in full costume—and the health of the foundress of the feast, the Sub-Prioress, was drank with enthusiastic plaudits. The presence of an *Amalthæan Horn* shed its novel and classic lustre on an Apician dessert, the perfection of which was only at odds with its profusion—

'The flood of feasting can no further flow!'"

It is evident from this that Mrs. Wightwick and some lady friends superintended and were present at this particular festival, and that it was a sort of *red-letter* event in the annals of the Order.

Whether or not the unusual excellence and prodigality of the last feast vexed the righteous souls of these jolly friars does not appear, but certain it is that at the next Conclave, held at the Refectory of Brother Bacon on November 13th, 1844, the whole matter was discussed; and it is recorded that "This Conclave was convened by a special præcept, in the form of a brief, issued by the Prior for the purpose of correcting certain aberrations and encroachments in the Refectorial and other Departments of the institution." The Precept is as follows:—

"BLUES!

THE PRIOR makes known that the next Blue Friarly Conclave will be holden at Brother Bacon's on Saturday the Ninth day of November next at Six o'clock p.m. precisely. [It was held on the 13th.]

THE PRIOR expressly wills the following to be a standing order, viz., that the Refreshments be such (and no other) as aforetime have been provided, to wit, Soup and Fish, a plain Joint, and a Pudding, Fruit *sine stint*, Wine *ad lib*. Provided always, that *Game, in the absence of all other viands*, be admissible.

THE BRETHREN are presumed to be perfectly aware of the ground on which this order is made; if not, it is sufficient that *the Prior Wills it*, and any B. F. found to trench upon or invade this regulation, even in a slight degree, will be subjected to a heavy penalty, and to the visits and sustention of the Brethren *de die in diem* until he be awakened to the propriety of strict observance.

As THE TIME is unusually short between the present date and the day fixed for the next meeting, THE PRIOR REMITS *on this one occasion* the production of a new Paper, and wills that, in lieu thereof, each Brother shall read one, to be selected from the Blue Box, which such Brother may have contributed during the first or second (but no later) year of the Institution; the Prior apprehending that the earlier productions of the Fraternity are now as little known to the Brethren themselves as to Blue Friars yet unborn.

THE PRIOR wills that the various Musical Instruments heretofore used at the Conclaves be found to be well tuned and otherwise in good order.

LASTLY; THE PRIOR has observed with deep concern that the Brethren do not separate when he, their Prior (who cannot err), sees fit to retire from the Conclave; The Prior therefore Wills that in future each Brother do withdraw to his own cell at Ten o'clock precisely; and if any one or more be found hereafter offending in this particular, the Prior will not only visit him or them severely, but the Blue Brother at whose cell the Conclave may be holden is hereby strictly enjoined under the like Penalty, to expel him or them by force, if attempting to linger after the hour now named.

(Signed)

20th October, 1844." TUCK.

What the instruments of music referred to consisted of we are not informed, except the incidental mention in the address to Brother Prism, previously noted. Doubtless they were in keeping with all the other items of the paraphernalia of the Order, or it may be that they consisted solely of the vocal organs of the members themselves; but possibly some light might be thrown on the matter by a reference to Brother Locke's paper, " Selections from the Blue Friar Orchestra," contributed to *Fraser's Magazine* in 1829; in the introduction to which he says : " It is not to be supposed that, when the Blue Brothers pass the bottle, they remain insensible to the charms of the musical glasses. Let the world understand, on the contrary, that they can ' rouse the night-owl with a catch,' and 'draw as many souls out of one weaver' as ever could their common uncle, famed Sir Toby Belch."

At the above Conclave, and in accordance with the Prior's Precept, the reading of original papers was dispensed with, owing to the short notice of the meeting, the brethren contenting themselves by dipping into the Blue Box and unearthing some of the earliest and choicest productions contributed in the first and second years of the Order.

The next entry is of a mournful character, being a record of the death of William Eastlake, a lay Brother of the Venerable Order, who was released from a life of bodily suffering on March 30th, 1845. A well-merited testimony to the virtues of his head and heart was contributed by Brother Locke, who, it appears, was the writer of several obituary notices of distinguished Plymouthians, which appeared from time to time in the columns of the local papers. From this honest testimony to the worth of a good and honoured man we make a few extracts :—

" The death of Mr. Eastlake merits more than the usual record of a weekly obituary. The lamented subject of our imperfect eulogy has peculiar claims upon us as the reporters of Plymouth's progressive history. In the intellectual records of the town his family name now does, and will hereafter, occupy a prominent position. Upon the moral excellences of Mr. Eastlake it would be impertinent to dwell. Upon his long suffering as an invalid, we would only rest so far as to say, that it has been the world's affliction as well as his own. The loss of Mr. Eastlake, as an intellectual man, is like that of a precious gem. Never was there a man who more broadly censured folly without any personal allusion to the individual committing it. And, in regard to his self-knowledge, we can most truly say, that, if it erred at all, it was on the side of a too modest concession to the self-sufficiency of others.

Mr. Eastlake's scholastic requirements were considerable. The multifarious powers of Shakspeare afforded him especial matter for comment, in which he delighted to indulge. Here he brought the lawyer's "niceness" to bear upon the dramatist's perfection. We need not remind our readers that Mr. Eastlake was the eldest brother of the pre-eminent artist of that name.* His conversations upon Art were not less remarkable than his comments on Literature. He professed no *technical* knowledge of Art: he was, in this respect, always a modest listener. He was the son of a remarkable father: and to that father's memory he always alluded with the most glowing feelings of filial submission and gratitude. Mr. Eastlake was a *politician* in the most extended sense of the term. We hesitate to call him of any *party*: though our own bias inclines us to regard him as a Whig . . . if the Whigs felt with him, it was rather their good fortune, than a matter of his seeking.

In spite of the severe asthmatic affection, which for many years, bore so heavily upon him, he delighted in the social communion of his friends. There was a singular buoyancy in his natural disposition, and the conflict between this and the depressing influences of his malady, left us under an equal sense of pleasure and of pain. While we feel the loss of much enjoyment and profit, we have at least the comfort of knowing that a good man has been released from much suffering. He will go to his grave, not full of years, but full of honours. He was one of the few links remaining connecting the old Plymouth with the new; and his departure suggests to us that we cannot be too mindful of the limited residue who are still left among us."

No further meeting was held until August 5th, 1845, when it is noted that the Silver Minor Seal of the Order,

---

* Sir Charles Locke Eastlake, President of the Royal Academy.

which had been ordered at a previous Conclave, and the new Conclave Box, were consecrated and consigned to the custody of the Prior and the Sacristan for the time being: a contribution of ten shillings being levied on each of the Brethren to meet the current expenses of the Order. At this Conclave the Refectorial programme was published in very original Latin, and the Brethren finished their *sederunt* by *whist*fully gazing on the portraits of certain Kings and Queens with their attendant knaves, each of whom had been *trumps* in their day, and up to an *odd trick* or two when put to it; which means of course that they betook themselves to sundry rubbers of whist. These solemn reflections on departed Royalty proved a wholesome practice for the fraternity, and was ordered to be continued at future Conclaves.

Refectorial Programme in original Latin,
WITH TRANSLATION APPENDED.

Cucumer cum Vino acido	𝔐𝔦𝔰𝔰𝔲𝔰 𝔓𝔯𝔦𝔪𝔲𝔰. Salmo / Battata Cocta / Decoctum ex Carnê Confectum	Butyrum liquefactum
Battata Cocta	𝔐𝔦𝔰𝔰𝔲𝔰 𝔖𝔢𝔠𝔲𝔫𝔡𝔲𝔰. Aniticulæ Assatæ (cum Salvia et Cepis) / Salinum Cœruleum / Coxa Agni	Pisi viridi
Caseus ex Lactario Chedderii	𝔐𝔦𝔰𝔰𝔲𝔰 𝔗𝔢𝔯𝔱𝔦𝔲𝔰. Clupeæ Encrasicolæ (cum segminis tosti panis) / Striblita Quadripartita / Fratrorum Cœruleorum	Panis bis Coctus

This is an exact copy of the Refectorial programme mentioned above, of which the following is given as a translation:—

Cucumber with Vinegar	**First Course.** Salmon Boiled Potatoes Gravy Soup	Melted Butter
Boiled Potatoes	**Second Course.** Roast Ducks (with Sage and Onions) Blue Salt Cellar Leg of Lamb	Green Peas
Cheddar Cheese	**Third Course.** Anchovy Toast Tart in four divisions	Biscuits

Before passing from the subject of *menus* it may be as well to include the following curious list, consisting of a series of cards found in the Blue Box:—

I AM
THE FIRST COURSE.
Happy Tawney Moor Soup.
Fish, without Head, Tail, Body, or Soul. N.B.—No Fins either.

I AM
THE SECOND COURSE.
Oxy-Hydro Beef Steaks. Curry Comb Fish Fowl.
A Stupendous Hog's Pudding; and a Powder Monkey.

I AM
THE THIRD COURSE.
Plumbago Pudding.
Sweets in Pairs. Clotilda Cream.

I AM
NO COURSE.
Mity Cheese; and a Good Salary.

WE ARE
OF COURSE
The Magpie and Owl in the Desert.

Amongst the miscellaneous papers contained in the Blue Box was that of which we here give a copy; but we find no entry in the Records to correspond—it is therefore probable that this " whip " had not the desired effect :—

"To LOCKE, BACON, AND ROGER.
These

WE, to whose wish succumb all other men's desires,
And *ex necessitate*, those of loyal true Blue Friars,
DEMAND of you, our Brethren, you urge no plea to 'scape, or
Fail forthwith to indite each one a racy B.F. Paper;
Which done, you're hereby bound, with promptness undiminish'd,
T' acquaint ourselves (our JOLLINESS) when you this work have finish'd;
When we, the fact admitting that Time and Tide are fleeting,
Will at some speedy season call in our grim cell a meeting;
For now of you 'tis said (meant doubtless to annoy ye),
On perd tout le tems ? qu' on peut mieux employer.

TUCK.   [*Seal*]
(The Prior)

Frankfort-on-the-Maine,
  Sept. 22—'45."

The Forty-second Grand Conclave of the Order was held at the Refectory of His Jolliness the Prior on August 13th, 1846, and proved to be the last, or at any rate no further record is made in the Blue Book, with the exception of entries relating to the deaths of other worthy members.

It will thus be seen that this club, or brotherhood, or Order, continued in existence for a period of seventeen years, and that its members met together in full Conclave no less than forty-two times, besides holding sundry other meetings for special purposes. There were contributed at these meetings an aggregate of about one hundred and fifty original papers, full of witty and wise sayings, sufficient to form a bulky volume; many of which we feel will be read with intense interest by the

Plymouthians of the present generation as the productions of men of the first rank in scientific and literary pursuits in the age in which they lived and laboured.

A list of all these papers will follow. The complete list of those which appeared in *Fraser's Magazine* will be found on pages 44-46. In the latter portion of our little volume will be found a selection of these papers, but our readers need scarcely to be reminded that the papers here given do not represent a tenth part of those witty productions which were contributed to the various conclaves of the Venerable Order of Blue Friars. We hope that sufficient interest will be taken in the present work to warrant the publication of a second volume, devoted exclusively to " Blue Friar Pleasantries."

It may interest our readers if we here give some extracts from the Treasurer's Book, covering the whole period of the operations of the Order. (The Sacristan, who acted as Treasurer and Secretary, was Mr. T. Duncan Newton.)

Extracts from the Treasurer's Book in account with the Blue Friars :—

1829. EXPENDITURE.

	£	s.	d.
May 18—Refectory Expences at Mount Batten	0	3	6
June 10—Crockery for the use of the Order	0	2	0
Four Pewter Plates	0	7	6
Four Pewter Chalices	0	8	0
Patent Gridiron	0	2	6
Three Bottles of Cider	0	1	6
Bread	0	1	0
Beefsteaks and Potatoes	0	3	1
12—Breakfasts, &c.	0	4	0
Car and Driver	0	16	6
Turnpikes	0	0	6
Secretary's and Treasurer's Books	0	14	6
Sigillum Monasticum Cœruleum	0	15	0
1830.			
Febry.—Paid Brother Locke for Impressions of Seal ..	0	3	0

Extracts from the Treasurer's Book.

		£	s.	d.
Febry.—Paid for Blue Box		0	13	0
Pair of Dies and two gross of B.F. Buttons		4	14	0
Sept. 20—Expences at Mount Batten		0	3	0
1831.				
March—Paid the Prior for Six Buffalo Spoons for the Order		0	7	6
July 11—Blue Teapot		0	2	0
Four Cups and Saucers		0	2	0
Victualling Bill on the expedition to Shag Bay		0	8	0
Six Teaspoons		0	1	0
Waterman		0	3	0
Collier's man		0	2	0
1832.				
January—Blue Chest		1	4	6
Painting same, &c.		0	6	8
Four Refectory Wine Glasses		0	4	0
July—Paid for making Silk Skull Caps in London		1	3	0
A Marinated Flaggon		0	4	0
Lush for the Cardinal		0	15	0
Half-ream of Paper		0	14	2
1833.				
March—16th share of a Ticket in the Glasgow Lottery		1	0	0
Nov. 23—Box for Brother Prism		0	2	3
Refectory Bill for ditto		2	11	6
Wines for ditto		2	4	6
Stuffing our Emblems		0	5	0
1835.				
July—Gross of B.F. Vest Buttons		0	18	0
1836.				
April—Two Refectory Platters		0	2	0
Two Refectory Chalices		0	3	6
May 20—Parchment Wrappers for B.F. Papers		0	2	0
Oct. 22—Hicks and Feather for B.F. Buttons		1	7	0
Champagne Emancipators		0	3	6
Relic of White Friary		0	1	6
Nov. 19—Carriage of Parcel to London		0	3	10
1840.				
Mch. 17—New Proboscos		0	3	0
New Caps		0	1	0
April—Thomas's Bill for Printing		0	9	6
October—The Cardinal's Sneezer		0	7	0

		£	s.	d.
1845.				
Jany. 14—Paid Arnold for new B.F. Tin Box	.. ..	0	10	0
Harris for painting same ..	.. .. ..	0	7	0
Jan. 29—Page's Bill for B.F. Seal ..	.. .. ..	3	16	0

The receipts consisted solely of contributions from the four original members, with two solitary exceptions, where "Somno" is credited with paying 5s. and 6s. respectively, but the name, although not the amount, is obliterated in a similar manner to the entries in the Blue Book.

The Chronicle of the Blue Friars is almost completed, only a mournful portion remaining, to wit, to notice briefly the final retirement of such of the Brethren who survived the decay of their Venerable Order.

On the 25th of April, 1866, His Jolliness, Tuck, the Prior of our Venerable Order of Blue Friars, and the "Noblest Roman of them all," resigned his latest breath to Him who gave it, at No. 5 Regent's Park, Exeter. A memoir was written by the Sub-Prior, Brother Locke, from which we think it desirable to make a few extracts to show the estimation in which this gentleman was held by his contemporaries:—

"THE LATE WILLIAM JACOBSON.

Mr. Jacobson was among the most remarkable of our local celebrities, at a time when Plymouth may be said to have been particularly distinguished by its number of clever and distinguished men; and not one of these but acknowledged him as of the brightest in the constellation. To the acumen that gave him high professional repute as a solicitor, he had talents that made some regret he had not been at the Bar; others, that the stage should not have benefited by his rich comic and imitative power; others, that his original genius for landscape art should not have been cultivated to the honour of the Water Colour Societies; but the society of Plymouth, abstractedly, certainly benefited the more by the circumstances which retained him as one of the choicest, if not indeed the very choicest of its spirits. He differed from others in a more than common reluctance to public display, and his more than indifference to

The Prior (Mr. William Jacobson).

public repute; nor even within the limited bounds of his immediate social circle did he choose to play 'the *Lion* of the party'; but where good taste received him on the strength of his character as a gentleman, with respect for his feelings, as they might be at the time, and with reference to his substantially valuable companionship, as it existed at *all* times, he would give out from the rich store of his entertaining powers in a manner not to be forgotten by his more intimate friends. Who of them now living (alas! how few), remember not his anecdotes of the Bar, his Jekelliana, his imitations of the old Judges, his *Mathewsian* reminiscences, his readings from the old comedies, and his life portraits of the old actors? His Munden, in the writer's estimation, was as close to the truth as it could be consistently, with more richness than even the original exhibited; his delivery of Lover's Irish Stories made Irishmen hold their sides; and it may be therefore well supposed that when he gave the 'humours' of Jacobson entire, they were entertaining indeed. Certain characters of the Plymouth of his youth were still his most taking presentments; and in his narration, whether spoken or written, the wit and accomplished refinement of the *man* were eminently conspicuous. . . . His feeling for art was far above the ordinary amount of critical pretension, and the poor artist of real genius was sure to find in him an appreciator and friend. . . . His judgment on the merits of a picture was indisputable, though he was even delicately careful to be silent only where he could not approve.

His right to judge was sufficiently attested in his own pretensions as an artist, which were far greater than his restraining modesty permitted him to set forth in his drawings; *i.e.*, he subdued himself to efforts, trivial in comparison with what another man with his ability would have exercised. Let those, however, who have a 'bit of Jacobson,' more particularly one of his 'dabs,' as he used to call them, look into its indications of feeling and mastery, and treasure it as a gem. There was some humour, too, in his art. The writer has by him a 'dab' of rock scenery, rich in the colours of decay, and weather beat, radiant in its 'sunset glow.' The suggestion was a fragment of an old Stilton cheese, but there is more of *might* in it than the insect of that name in pronunciation. The scenery of Devon is assuredly inspiring enough, and Jacobson could have illustrated Carrington's poems with pictures most embellishing.

One quality in the mind of him who is now the subject of our heartfelt eulogy, was its *appreciative* sensibility. The vanity of self-estimate was never less seen than in him; nor a generosity in the estimate of others, more. So strongly did he manifest his admiration, and express his eulogies, that he became occasionally subject to the charge of affecting more than he felt, and of saying more than he believed of the merits of his participators in favour. Serious accusation, indeed! Yet one to which he might have pleaded 'guilty,' in the assurance of a 'recommendation to *mercy*' from his jury, and a sentence of acquittal from his judge. In truth, he was not one of your 'speak-my-mind' people; but out of *some* people's *heart* the *mouth* speaketh; and of these was William Jacobson. His delight was to see his friends appreciated; and to remain himself in the background—as long as his admirers would allow. On one order of occasion, at least, he showed himself the reverse of a flatterer; and that was when any worldly advantage to himself might be flattery's result. At such times a reserve, verging on forbidding moodiness, would appear; only equalled by the evidence of his offended pride, when the uncomplimentary flattery of the vulgar or the thoughtless had for its mere object the engagement of his entertaining powers.

He was not a man to be made *use* of, and 'told to be funny'; nor to put up with 'hail fellow, well met' familiarities. In the society of 'sage, grave men' he was no less at home than in that of the cheerful and witty refined. His presence, indeed, was in its repose singularly grave; nor was there ever a finer head than his for the shoulders of a judge. This was so remarkable that even his mock gravity had an effect almost suppressing the smile it was intended to raise. Like the burlesque acting of Robson, it was nearly as impressive as the reality burlesqued. The writer of this has his portrait as he appeared some fifteen years ago; his curling light hair forming a kind of *nimbus* over his lofty and spacious brow; and the expression of the eyes and mouth exactly giving his character as that of one of high moral perceptions, quick sensibilities; 'a wit himself, and the causer of wit in others'; his own powers in perfect repose, and his appreciative recipiency shewn in a state of generous happiness. Mr. Jacobson was born long before very many of his fellow townsmen, whom he long out-lived; and until in his eighty-fifth year, there was much probability of his living much longer. It may be an amiable folly, if not something less excusable, to desire the prolongation of years, in *suffering*, but it had become an earnest hope, that *such* a remarkable instance of bodily strength and mental preservation should be yet long retained to us. To lose such an aged man (for the expression '*old* man,' seems scarcely correct) is to lose a Cypress tree that is green among the leafless younger trees around. It is more than a common loss to the Winter Garden.

But WILLIAM JACOBSON is gone! and the comfort of those who

loved him, and had his love, is this:—Though 'he shall not return to me, I shall go to him.' Meanwhile, as 'a thing of beauty is a joy for ever' (what a piece of scripture has that sentence by Keats become!), so the fact of having known such a man as he we now lament, is for ever a 'joy.' That knowledge and its pleasantness

'Still will keep
A bower quiet for us, and a sleep
Full of sweet dreams, and health and quiet breathing.
Therefore, on every morrow, are we breathing
A flow'ry band to bind us to the earth,
Spite of despondence, of the inhuman dearth
Of noble natures, of the gloomy days,
Of all the unhealthy and o'er-darken'd ways
Made for our searching: yes, in spite of all,
Some *shape* of beauty moves away the pall
From our dark spirits.'

A little while, and pleasing thoughts of William Jacobson, as we knew him living, will move away the 'pall' of sorrow for a loss which is his gain; and, while he is beginning to live the life that has no end, we can make him live again the old life by the magic of imagination operating on memory."

Many interesting reminiscences of the "Prior" are still treasured up by his old friends and associates, the recital of which would fill a volume; we must therefore content ourselves with inserting in their proper place in this book a few of the witty papers contributed to the Blue Friar Conclaves by Mr. Jacobson. His widow (third wife) the late Mary Grace Furneaux Jacobson, survived him many years, and died at Woodland Terrace, Plymouth, on the 8th April, 1878. She was never tired of extolling his memory, or of relating the pleasant gatherings which took place at their house, both during their residence at Taunton and at Plymouth.

From this accomplished lady the writer of these pages has received from time to time many valuable hints and much encouragement to persevere in literary pursuits. It is, however, a matter for regret that the oft-repeated promise of an examination of the books and papers of her late husband was never realized, and that on her death a large mass of valuable biographical material was either destroyed or scattered amongst the miscellaneous buyers at a public auction, who could scarcely be expected to interest themselves in such matters. A few relics only survived this dispersion; and these consist of volumes of MS. kindly placed in our hands by Mr. G. F. Radmore, the executor of the late Mrs. Jacobson; but beyond containing copies of some of his Blue Friar papers, and a few of his songs, they are of little value from a literary point of view. The mention of Mr. Jacobson's songs recalls the fact that the late Mrs. Jacobson was an accomplished musician, and that she set several of her husband's charming lyrics to music. She herself was the writer of many sweet and pretty trifles, besides being a critic of no mean order. We give a few of Mr. Jacobson's songs here, as they could not rightly be included amongst the "Blue Friar Pleasantries."

SONG—"Sigh not for Me."

Sigh not for me—
The day that Fancy touch'd is past,
Its brilliant hues too bright to last,
And I am sunk beneath life's blast:
Sigh not for me.

Speak not of me—
Nor seek to check the ready tongue,
Where once the kindest accents hung,
But foremost now to do me wrong:
Speak not of me.

Think not of me—
Soon, soon shall earth this favor'd frame
Conceal from all that praise or blame,
And shed oblivion o'er my name:
Think not of me!

W. J.

SONG.

O think no more that hope can cheer,
  Or joy this sorrowing bosom warm :
Go, pour thy vows in other's ear,
  For me they may no longer charm.

The tree by Winter's blast borne down,
  Can hail no more the cheering sun ;
And since I've ill deserved thy frown,
  I cannot by thy smile be won.

William Jacobson.

TO ———.

Sair and wearie gae the hours,
  Jessie, sair and wearie ;
Life seems reft of a' its flowers,
  When fra' thee, my dearie.

When fra' thee auld Time his san'
  Sparely seems to measure ;
But, when wi' thee, speeds his han',
  Envious o' my pleasure.

O wad Fortune ance incline
  To grant thy Friend a boon,
I wadna' riches should be mine,
  Nor ask a monarch's crown.

I'd hae the drearie moments a'
  Sae bright and blissfu' be
As those which sweetly steal awa'
  When, Jessie dear, wi' thee !

W. J.

The versatility of the Prior may be gathered from the following impromptu poetical epistle addressed to " William S. Harris, Esq., Surgeon, Union Street, Plymouth." It bears no date, but was evidently occasioned by the postponement through inclement weather of some excursion which the Brethren had been looking forward to, probably in 1829 or 1830, as Mr. Nicholas Lockyer, who is mentioned, was Mayor at that time.

I'll tell you what, Bacon,
('Tis a saying in Lacon),
Who for lobster, crab, cockle, or eel,
In such weather from shed
Would pop out his head,
Had need be a mermaid or seal.

But as I am neither,
And so wet is the weather
(The wind blowing stronger and stronger),
I'm for staying at home
Until fairer time come
To catch cockle and eke *caper longer*.

There's not the least chance
That the elements' dance
Will be o'er for to-morrow's excursion,
So the plan I renounce
(Best to do so at once—
Suspense is but sorry diversion).

Now list the command
From our own proper hand,
And a line by a messenger, quick,
To say how we feel
About shell-fish and eel,
To that cock of good cocks, Captain Nick.

And tell him, as Mayor,
Since he cannot be there
T' affect, as proposed, our vagary,
That by law he's a right
To amend our sad plight,
And summon them all from the Lairy.

By the hand of a Friar,
(Or, oath that is higher,
By the blue fists of him who's the luck
Your Prior to be)
If well *gesserit se*,
I lament this affair.
     FATHER TUCK.

 P.S.—
Cease, O cease the 'tato stew,
Cease the whisky punch to brew,

Brother Bacon (SIR WILLIAM SNOW HARRIS, Kt., F.R.S.)

> Sport the sheep, and graze the cow,
> (Chops nor steaks are wanted now),
> Swim the duck in pond or pool,
> Nor Bacon. Locke, nor little ——,
> No, nor Tuck, tho' last not least,
> Occasion have for bird or beast.

The last entry in the Blue Book records the death, on January 22nd, 1867, of Brother Bacon, "the second Brother of our Venerable Order by seniority, who closed his useful career in this world, full of well deserved honours. His mortal remains are deposited in a vault at the upper northern end of the Public Cemetery, Plymouth."

Several interesting and highly eulogistic newspaper cuttings are inserted in the Records respecting Sir William Snow Harris (Brother Bacon), from which, if space permitted, some acceptable quotations might be made. But he was so well known, both as a man of science and a member of the leading literary institution of Plymouth,* that any lengthened statement regarding him and his works would be superfluous. The following general outline may therefore be deemed sufficient:—

"Sir William Snow Harris was a distinguished physicist, a member of the Royal College of Surgeons, and a Fellow of the Royal Society. He was born at Plymouth in 1792, and devoted himself through life to researches in physical science. In June, 1831, he was admitted a Fellow of the Royal Society; in 1835 he received the Copley Medal; in 1841, an acknowledgment from the Civil List for his scientific discoveries; in 1845, he received two honorary presents from the Emperor of Russia; and was knighted by her Majesty in 1847. He expired at his residence, 6 Windsor Villas, Plymouth, on January 22nd, 1867, in his seventy-sixth year. His death, which was owing to no settled form of disease, but rather to a general breaking up of the system, has deprived the upper circle of Plymouth society of one of its brightest ornaments. He was not only a man of scientific

---

* The Plymouth Institution, before whose members the Lecture on the Blue Friars was delivered, March 28th, 1889.

attainments and practical industry, but also a man of genius, of a versatile and originative aptitude. Even towards art he had some tendency, and there is sufficient evidence of the fluency of his pen in the lighter varieties of prose and verse. For music he had an enthusiasm. To ordinary hearers he was a clever performer on the pianoforte and harp, and was of considerable service in assisting in the musical instruction of his children. His conversational ability rendered him alike welcome among serious arguers or playful humorists. His gravity was the very opposite of ' oracular solemnity,' but nothing offended him more than ill-timed frivolity, unless it be the inflated pretension which could not descend to fun and frolic. Sir William began his manhood's career as a militia surgeon, and subsequently practised the surgical and medical profession at Plymouth; but his curative skill was rather sought by trusting patients than exercised by him with any anxious desire for fame or emolument. The pursuit of electrical science soon became the great object of his mind. His name will ever be popularly associated with the lightning conductor. The scientific papers of Sir W. S. Harris are very numerous, besides his work on ' Thunderstorms' and an ' Elementary Treatise on Electricity.' He also effected considerable improvements in the mariner's compass. A naval man once observing a sailing boat tacking about in the Sound, exclaimed, ' Egad, the fellow in that boat well knows what he's about.' The 'fellow' was W. Snow Harris, F.R.S. He is still remembered by many, in his sailor-like jacket, ample trousers, and shoes,—the very ideal of that sort of man who, of all in the town, might leave his dignity to take care of itself, under whatever fashion it might appear. Many were his phases; but in one phase we believe he was never seen; he was never beheld on horseback; and it is doubtful if he ever danced a hornpipe. We may record the description given of him by the late Capt. N. Lockyer, who said, ' Harris is like a barrel organ; you may set him to any tune.' The memory of Sir William as a man of extreme tenderness will long be cherished by those on whom, when he had ceased from ordinary medical practice, he still attended; he was friend, doctor, and nurse, as no one but he could have been. His latter sufferings and deprivations must have been severe indeed to one with a mind unimpaired; but they were borne as though the culture of physical science had involved that of moral philosophy, and as if the growth of pious resignation had accompanied the decay of temporal vitality. The departure of Sir William Harris is that of one who has exercised the talents committed to him, and who otherwise lived as a gentle and Christian-minded man."

(Brother Locke.)

We have thus followed several of the founders of the Order of Blue Friars to their last resting-place, and little more remains to be said.

Brother Locke (Mr. Wightwick) removed from Plymouth many years ago, and settled at Clifton, but continued an honorary member of the Plymouth Institution down to the time of his death, which took place at Portishead, near Bristol, in 1872. He is best known as the author of the "Palace of Architecture," but his other architectural works equally deserve our consideration. He is well remembered by many Plymouthians now living; one gentleman, a member of the Plymouth Institution, says, "I knew him well, but always in connection with the Artists and Amateurs' Society, of which he was a member, frequently attending our evening meetings, and sketching with a reed pen, at which he was very clever (buildings of course). I also knew him as a reader of Shakespeare, and remember him as a reader of Ruskin, at the Athenæum, after which occurred a most animated, if not a fierce discussion respecting the merits of Turner's works, *versus* Claude, and in this Mr. Norman, father of Alfred Norman, Colonel Hamilton-Smith, and Mr. A. Johns, the artist, took the principal parts. It was Wightwick and Johns for Turner, against Norman and Smith for Claude. Shortly after this Wightwick lent me Ruskin's "Modern Painters," 1st vol., which was the first time I saw it."[*] Mr. Wightwick was also the author of two plays, and a contributor to several west country magazines, of one of which[†] he was editor, and to which he was also an extensive contributor.

The following brief sketch of the life of George Wight-

---

[*] Mr. Philip Mitchell.
[†] "The Philo-Danmonian."

wick, with a list of his principal works, has been furnished by his widow (second wife) now, and for many years, resident at Clifton, Bristol. It will doubtless be read with interest by many of his old friends and acquaintances:—

"George Wightwick (Fellow of the Royal Institute of British Architects), born at Mold, in Flintshire, August 26th, 1802. His father, William Wightwick, was a country gentleman, and inherited a small estate at Albrighton, in Staffordshire. He sold this and bought a place called Alyn Bank, near Mold, and married Anna Maria, daughter of George Taylor, a portrait painter. Her grandfather's name was Mortimer, and he wrote a History of England.

William Wightwick was drowned in a canal, near Mold, when going home one dark night. His son (George Wightwick) was then only 9 years old, and was the only surviving child. His mother soon left Alyn Bank, and in three years' time married Mr. Damant of the Stock Exchange.

George Wightwick was educated (chiefly) at Wolverhampton Grammar School, where he was a boarder, and at Tooting School. He afterwards studied architecture under Mr. Lapidge and Sir John Soane.

At the age of 25 he made a tour in Italy, staying in Rome four months, in Florence two, and at Venice one month. On his return to England he married Caroline, daughter of Mr. Damant by his first wife, and settled at Plymouth in partnership with Mr. Foulston, in the year 1828, I believe.

He was very successful in his profession, and retired in 1851, when he removed to Clifton, where he resided four years. After this he and his wife (who had been a sufferer to gradual paralysis for many years) went to live at Portishead, Somerset. In 1859 (I think) Mr. Wightwick made a tour in search of health to Gibraltar, Granada, and the neighbouring places, being greatly interested in the Alhambra, of which he commenced a large drawing, unfortunately never finished.

His wife died in 1867, and in the following year he married Isabella, eldest daughter of Samuel Jackson, landscape painter, of Clifton. Mr. Wightwick died on the 9th of July, 1872, and was interred at Portishead. There were no children.

Mr. Wightwick was highly talented and industrious, and did a considerable amount of writing and lecturing even after his retirement. He was a profound student of Shakspeare, and gave numerous readings of his plays in public as well as at his own house and those of friends. He also lectured on architecture. He possessed brilliant powers of conversation, with an unusual amount of wit, which made him a great favourite in society. His nature was upright and kindly.

Mr. Wightwick's principal literary works were:—' Palace of Architecture '; ' Hints to Young Architects ' (a new edition of which was published a few years ago); ' Life of an Architect ' (his own), published in Bentley's Miscellany, from 1855 to 1858; ' Essay on the Architecture and Genius of Sir Christopher Wren,' written in 1859, for which he received a silver medal; ' Blue Friar Pleasantries,' which appeared in *Fraser's Magazine* from 1837 to 1840; ' The Life and Remains of Wilmot Warwick,' 2 vols. (1829); ' The Tin Box'; ' Guide to Plymouth, Stonehouse, and Devonport' (Nettleton, 1836); ' Blacklock Forest ' (this was the last of Mr. Wightwick's writings; it came out in Colburn's *New Monthly Magazine*, about 1870). While residing at Plymouth he wrote some very amusing Comic Songs, and used to sing them to his own accompaniment on the piano; he also wrote two Plays—Henry II. and Richard I.; various papers on Shakespeare's Plays; and numerous other works, chiefly on architecture.*

Some of his paintings were:—A collection of large water-colour views of the antiquities of Rome (left by will to the Royal Institute of British Architects); two very fine views of Venice, presented to the same (after his death) by Mrs. Wightwick; a number of large sepia drawings used in his lectures on architecture, etc.

On leaving Plymouth in 1851, he was presented by the builders of that town with a handsome silver inkstand, which he always regarded with great satisfaction.

Burke's ' History of the Landed Gentry ' contains an account of the Wightwick family, none of whom seem to remain in Staffordshire at the present time. It is a very old family. The Mortimers trace their descent from the Earl of March."

A propos of Mr. Wightwick, the following extract from a letter by an old and esteemed friend, Mr. J. N. Bennett, of Plymouth, may be of interest to our readers, as showing us one side of the character of this noteworthy man :—

" In the years 1851-2, an association was formed in this town under the name of the Plymouth Church Reform Association; its object

---

* It will be noticed that Mr. Wightwick's contributions to *Fraser's Magazine*, were considerably in excess of the other members of the Blue Friars' Brotherhood.

being to discountenance the advance of what is now called Ritualism in the Church of England. On the occasion of the formation of the Society, Mr. Wightwick applied to the Secretary (Mr. J. C. Bellamy) to be enrolled among its members, but as Mr. Wightwick was not a common or even frequent attendant at any Church of England place of worship, some doubts were expressed as to his eligibility. I was desired to see him on the subject and to ascertain his views. I called on him accordingly, and had a very pleasant conversation with him on the point involved. He fully admitted that he was not formally attached to any religious community, but that he was nevertheless a firm believer in Holy Scripture, its inspiration and authority, but that he failed to find in the worship of the Church of England (of which he said he professed to be a member) that conformity to the simple and earnest teaching of the Gospel set forth in the Scriptures; and that he desired to see such a reformation of the Church as would exclude the appendages of mediæval and modern times. Mr. Wightwick then rose from his chair, and went to another room, from which he presently returned bearing a large (I think quarto) book in his hands, which proved to be a note-book in his own handwriting, containing his own comments, especially on the four Gospels, expressed in terms of deep reverence for the Word of God, and the pleasure he enjoyed in contemplating its mysteries. Mr. Wightwick accordingly became a member of the Society, which afterwards published lectures and pamphlets by its members on the subject of their theories."

Mrs. Wightwick, in her biographical notes which appear on a former page, mentions the fact that her husband wrote some comic and other songs and pieces, in addition to his published works and his contributions to the "Blue Friar Pleasantries." Among these may be mentioned the following, contained in a volume of "Canticles by Locke, B.F.," evidently privately printed:—

"The Steam-boat." Dedicated to Captain Nichols, of the *Sir Francis Drake*.
"The Play." ("The Play—the Play's the Thing.")
"Philosophers' Hall."
"The Good-natured Fellow."
"A Song on the Sea"; being a Parody on Barry Cornwall's Song.
"The Rejected! A Song in the Modern Sentimental Style."
"Overture. A Musico-Graphical Ode."

"Why? An Interrogatory Chant."
"The Launch of the *Nile*."
"The Mystery of the Box Tunnel."

Mr. W. F. Collier, in his very interesting *brochure* entitled "William Robert Hicks, of Bodmin" (Brendon, Plymouth, 1888), thus refers to Wightwick:—

"One of Hicks's early and best friends was George Wightwick, a man much sought after as a fine talker, a good story teller, and one of the best readers of Shakespeare's plays that ever read to the public.

In speaking of Hicks I must give a passing glance at his fellow wit. George Wightwick, of Plymouth, a friend of Macready's, was architect of the Lunatic Asylum at Bodmin, of which Hicks was the Governor, and he was one of the first to bring Hicks into notoriety. Wightwick was an enthusiast, and a great appreciator of merit in others. He was delighted with Hicks's fun, and put him forward as the most amusing person to be found in the West of England. Wightwick, as well as Hicks, was a well-known man throughout the West of Devon and Cornwall, and was much sought after as an entertainer of fellow guests at those most delightful parties at country houses, where many meet for a day or two in the mansion of a country gentleman. Perhaps there is nothing in the world so pleasant as a large party gathered together in an English country house—a fine old mansion situated in beautiful scenery—where every luxury is at command, and true hospitality well understood. Wightwick and Hicks in such company, with their talk, their stories, and their music —they were both songsters—would be in themselves luxuries of the highest order. The two celebrities told stories of one another.

Hicks used to tell stories of one Captain Blank. I must use unreal names, that I may not hurt the feelings of living persons, descendants or relations of the heroes of the stories, and I must pick out the commonest names in order to avoid identification, though the real Cornish names will be a great loss. Hicks told many absurd stories of this Captain Blank, a mining captain. The title of 'Captain' is a very favourite one in Cornwall, and is always bestowed on miners in authority. Wightwick, having heard many stories of Captain Blank, met him one day when in company with Hicks in Cornwall. Wightwick, with his usual enthusiasm, went up to Captain Blank and shook him warmly by the hand, saying, 'How are you, Captain Blank? I am delighted to see you.' He was received with a cold, astonished stare, Captain Blank by no means partaking in the warmth of feeling exhibited by Wightwick. On which Wightwick said,

'Captain Blank, my name is Wightwick.' Captain Blank looked at him with great deliberation, and slowly answered, 'I never heard of 'ee !' "

Yet another biographical notice must be given, of a gentleman who, although not a prominent Blue Friar, is yet mentioned on several occasions, and was elected a Lay Brother at an early stage of the history of the Fraternity. The short notice of John Collier which follows has been prepared by his son, Mr. William F. Collier :—

"John Collier, the son of John Collier, was born in the old house 53 Southside Street, Plymouth, on the 2nd March, 1769. He succeeded his father in his business when very young, and carried it on as a Plymouth merchant to his death in 1849. He was a merchant during the whole of the great French war in the latter end of the last and the beginning of the present centuries. His parents, his brother and sisters were members of the Society of Friends, staunch Quakers, but at an early age he was read out of the Society for disobedience to their rules. He retained various Quaker opinions through the whole of his life, and would never have any share whatever in privateers, many of which were owned in Plymouth in the war time and committed depredations on the enemy. This port being the first in the Channel and the safest, prizes were brought here in great numbers, and John Collier's principal business then was the sale and disposal of prize cargoes for account of the owners under adjudication by the Admiralty Courts. It was a very busy stirring time at Plymouth, and the earliest records of the Chamber of Commerce show an astonishing extent and variety of imports, consisting of the prize cargoes. In early life John Collier formed an intimate friendship with Captain Andrew Saunders, R.N., after whom our good citizen, Mr. Andrew Saunders Harris, takes his name. Captain Saunders was an accomplished well-read man, and had been honoured with a medal for an invention connected with the Royal Navy. Captain Saunders was a philosopher, and the young John Collier acquired from him opinions which he held through life. Captain Thomas Saunders left him his library, and may be said to have exercised a great influence on his career.

John Collier was from his earliest days a Liberal of the Liberals, and was the first in Plymouth to cut his long hair and wear a crop, for which the boys in the street hooted him. It was supposed then to be a sign of sympathy with the great French Revolution. He strongly opposed the old Corporation, as they were called, in their management of the water, Drake's leat being a very old bone of contention, but when the Municipal Corporation Act, 1835, was passed, he said the ratepayers had power to manage their own property, and he need no longer interfere. He acted as chairman in the great Reform agitation, which ended in the Reform Act, 1832, and presided at a monster meeting on the Hoe, when the people were in a great state of excitement. He was in consequence returned unopposed, with the late Mr. Bewes, of Beaumont, as first members of Parliament for Plymouth under the Reform Act, and sat from that time to 1841, when he resigned with Mr. Bewes, a period of nine years, during which they successfully fought two contested elections in the Liberal interest.

John Collier was a Plymouth man, of an old Plymouth family, but he was from his youth fond of sport and of country life. He was in his time a good fisherman, and a good shot, and in his early days made his own fishing rods, and the stocks of his own guns. During the whole of his life he never had a day's illness, and he often said he had never been in bed a day. He never retired from business, but he passed some of his time latterly at his country seat, Grimstone. He did his last day's work the day before he died. He was never Mayor of Plymouth, but he was an Alderman for some years, up to the time of his death.

We may here introduce some lines composed by the Brethren, and headed thus :—

THE CELEBRATED LAMENT
COMPOSED BY
Tuck (the Prior),
Locke (the Sub-Prior),
Bacon, and
Roger (the Clerk and Sacristan),
On the Departure of the Chaplain of the Order (the Rev. J. H. Macaulay) from Plymouth ;
Delivered September 17th, 1832.

Go mourn, oh thou learned Athenæum ;
Lament, oh ye sellers of brooms ;
Freemasons who haunt the Lyceum,
Haste, shut up your windows and rooms.

For he's gone with his learned quotations,
At Repton's famed villa to fix,
And by swallowing strong Latin potations
With the dust of past ages to mix.
   He is gone with his Greek and his Graces,
   With his hic, and his hæc, and his hoc,
   And Plymouth no longer embraces
   Macaulay, that jolly good cock.

No voice in that Hall is resounding
Which the student in Classics attracts,
And which, with a power astounding,
Proclaims to the world 'tis Almack's.
That voice which is mellow as honey,
Loud as thunder, yet smooth as a leek,
Which can turn, in the twirl of a penny,
An Englishman into a Greek.
   For he's gone with his Greek, etc.

What magic has caused all this pother,
What Fairy has hurried him hence;
Oh, where shall we look for another
To fill up the vacuum immense.
We can't look to Coleridge or Luney,
To Byrth or to solemn Sam Rowe—
The best of them all is a spooney
At bending Ulysses's bow.
   For he's gone, etc.

He was all you could wish after dinner:
He never was down in the dumps;
There was never a happier sinner
When he picked up a handful of trumps.
He filled all the fair with devotion,
To his pulpit came every gay lass,
The attraction which caused the emotion
Was nearly as great as the mass.
   But he's gone, etc.

He was learned, and lively, and lazy:
The daylight oft peep'd on his pate,
His speeches would sometimes amaze ye
When he talked of reforming the State.

No Whig ever made such orations
In the Hall, or the street, or the room,
The Tories ne'er got such jobations
From Ebrington, Russell, or Brougham.
   But he's gone, etc.

His wit was as fresh as sweet-briar,
And bright as a midsummer's day;
He ought to have been a Blue Friar,
But the Freemasons walked him away.
But the Friars still hope to reclaim him
From sun, moon, and stars, and all that;
And if pride should not too much inflate him
May yet tip him a Cardinal's hat.
   Tho' he's gone with his Greek and his glory,
   Mid the dust of past ages to sit,
   And if he should never turn Tory
   It won't be for lack of the wit.
                    Brother Bacon (Harris).

He's gone with his Irish high-dried,
Bolangaro, old Paris, rappee,
With a box in each pocket supplied,
And sometimes, 'tis said, two or three.
Whatever the taste we professed
He had always the snuff that could mate us.
If he wanted a motto, the best
'Tis agreed 'twould be *semper paratus*.
Enjoyment that's past time endears,
And now, alas! brought to a close is
His talk that so tickled our ears,
His snuff that so tickled our noses.
                    Prior Tuck (Jacobson).

Alas! that the flower of critics
No longer should bloom in the Square,
I have sought him at Newton's and Wightwick's,
I can find him—nor here—no, nor there.
Then where, and oh! where the deuce is he?
Shades of Sophocles, Æschylus, tell;
Euripides, if you're not busy,
My burning anxiety quell.

For I fear he's gone to be married;
If so, he's a jerry for life,—
I know what it is to be harried
With that old theme of dread—a young wife.
Ne'er again his whole length he'll repose on
His sofa from heel tap to head,
He will never again freely doze on
The diagonal line of his bed.

Ah! Praed, tho' your verses flow featly,
From his lips more melodious they pour,
Nor was fair Aramintha so sweetly
Addressed by her cousin before.
No more shall the cause of the Drama
Resound in Athenian Hall,
His dilations upon the Digamma
No longer shall puzzle us all.

'Tis a subject that needs must be wept on.
How uncertain are temporal joys!
He spurns Plymouth to settle at Repton—
Devon Beauties for Derbyshire Toys.
But has he, then, left us for ever?
Will he never again grace the Hoe?
The courteous—the classic—the clever—
My own Aramintha, say "No!"

Locke (Wightwick).

He's *not* gone; he's not *going*; he *shan't* go.
'Twill break my poor heart if he does.
I'll write, and I'll tell him he *can't* go,
They shan't have my own lusty coz.
What the deuce do they want with Macaulay?
He's too good for Repton by far.
Let them fetch him, and whate'er may befall me,
We'll try Devon 'gainst Derbyshire *spar*.

Is it nothing to lose—p'raps for ever—
Our champion of learning and fun?
Can they send in his stead one so clever
Weighing anything like *Twenty stone*?
From me may all attempts far be
Of raking up things for the nonce,

But shew me a man throughout Derby
Wearing *three* pocket napkins at once !
I've tried to believe I'm mistaken,
And that Almack's will open once more ;
But no! Friars Locke, Tuck, and Bacon,
Have left us no hope on that score !
Well! since he must go to Repton,
I'll only survive it to-night,
I'll find out the bed he last slept on,
And die—if I don't, blow me tight.

Roger (Newton).

Mr. Wightwick designed a monument to the Dartmoor poet, Carrington, an illustration of which appeared in the *South Devon Monthly Museum* for September, 1833. It was in the form of a cromlech, and was to be composed of Dartmoor granite, of as few blocks as might be allowed by the fixed scale of magnitude. The proposal was to erect this monument on the Hoe, where the Camera Obscura lately stood, and commanding at once three prominent subjects of Carrington's muse, viz.—Dartmoor, Plymouth Sound, and Mount Edgcumbe. But this, like many other happily conceived ideas, was never carried out, and the only memorial to this highly-gifted Devonshire poet, is the solitary stone inscribed with his name and date of death on the summit of the eminence overlooking the Dewer Stone, above "the brawling Cad."

Many other matters of interest might be enumerated respecting "Brother Locke," but we refrain, lest our biographical notes should become too lengthy in proportion to the extent of the book.

We regret to say that up to going to press with this sheet the biographical particulars of the other members of the Order, Edwin Lovell, Thomas Duncan Newton, and others, have not been received ; they must therefore be reserved for an Appendix, to follow such of the "Pleasantries" as may be included in the present volume.

But before proceeding to the "Pleasantries," or rather that portion of the Blue Friar papers which appeared in *Fraser's Magazine*, with others, hitherto unpublished, we propose to add a few odds and ends which we have gathered from the Blue Box and other sources, which are collateral with the Records and therefore of interest to our readers. The first of these to which we would call attention is entitled "The Private View," and has reference, we presume, to a picture by Mr. Ball, described in the extract which follows:—

THE PRIVATE VIEW.

Read in Conclave, April 19th, 1833.

The favored few now see the picture,
Each critic whispers praise or stricture.
See the sage lecturers grouped together,
No altar-piece was e'er so clever.
Bless me! the Lord High Admiral's standing,
The solemn scene his eye commanding,
The empty chair, so like a throne,
A Prince might deign to sit upon.
No seat on earth gives such delight—
How Saints and Sinners, Thursday night,
If President were then t' vacate it,
Would stare, and know not how to take it—
But Royal Tars, with hearts of oak,
Think ceremony all a joke;
Besides, to him who rules a Nation
Philosophy's all Botheration.

Harris has proved, it is confessed,
That *some* wise men are in the West;
Henceforth, no thunderbolt shall shiver
Bowsprit or mast, in sea or river.
Sailors thank God; and fill their glasses,
While to the deep the lightning passes—

Safe, ship and crew, oh! heavenly pleasure,
Thus to preserve life's sacred treasure:
Admiring nations, Harris, praise thee,
Thy country should to honours raise thee!

Ladies, I pray you, not too near,
The breathing canvas ill can bear
The piercing eyes of critics fair.
Say, has the pencil well portrayed
Of Plymouth Stars each form and grade
Of minds, each character and shade?
"Yes," Celia cries; "but how distressing
That such a painter wants the blessing
Of partner dear, to make his tea,
To cook his chops, his model be,
To stretch his canvas, brushes clean,
To scrape his palette, morn or e'en;
A peerless model she would prove
To share his name, requite his love.
No perfect being shall we find him
Till silken chains in wedlock bind him;
Inspired by Beauty, we predict
He must become a Benedict.
What Adam was, before the fall,
So will be then the painter B——!

Mr. Ball's Picture of the King's Visit to the Athenæum.

Well may we hope for the immortality of Mr. Ball's picture, when we consider how many of us it will immortalize. Then shall our Athenæum be as familiar in classic memory as the "School of Athens," and the Recorder of Plymouth go down to posterity with the Royal Reformer of England. To the naval world it must ever remain a subject of interest, since its prominent features are those of the Sailor King, and of him to whose philosophic zeal our ship will owe their safety from the thunderbolt.

As to the merits of the picture in a critical point of view, we must, in the first place, admit the extreme difficulty of giving artistical treatment to a subject of the kind, where the chief purpose is a series of portraits, and the chief desire of every sitter a prominent situation in the group. This considered, Mr. Ball has done well: he has varied the position of the numerous countenances as much as the presence of royalty can be supposed to admit; for Lord High Admirals of the Guelph family are not found in the Athenæum every day; and when they do appear, it must be expected that they will prove more attractive than plaster casts. The faces, therefore, for the most part are directed towards the Duke of Clarence (now our King: God save him!), and among these are many excellent likenesses. The portraits given (besides those of the King, Sir Byam Martin, &c.) are of the President of the Institution and proprietor of the picture; Messrs. Norman, Johns, E. Gandy, H. Gandy and son, Col. Hamilton Smith, Dr. Cookworthy, the Rev. Messrs. Lampen, Rowe, Luney, Coleridge, Byrth and Macaulay; Messrs. Prance, Prideaux, Wightwick, Fuge, Eastlake, Gill, Coryndon; Drs. Hingston and E. Moore, with a striking likeness of the painter himself, and an accurate resemblance of the President's seat and northern end of the Athenæum hall, forming a bold and beautiful background. Upon the varying strength of resemblance in the portraits, persons will, of course, differ, but, taken collectively, all beholders will, no doubt, agree in allowing that Mr. Ball has proved himself fully equal to the important task of combining truth of *expression* with accuracy of *feature*. The general aspect of the picture is rich and harmonious; nor need we hesitate to affirm, that Mr. Ball, already far advanced, has made another considerable step in his professional career.

The existence of the picture is alike flattering to the numerous members of the Plymouth Institution represented, and honourable to its liberal and enlightened proprietor. A good specimen is added to the catalogue of English Art, and great hope excited as to the future progress of the artist.—*South Devon Monthly Museum*, Vol. II., 1833, pp. 46-47.

The following tribute to the memory of a remarkable man (from the pen of George Wightwick) will doubtless be read with interest:—

THE LATE JOHN LEECH.

Where is the eye, whose joy has been to gaze
On forms of beauty, in the potent strength
Of Woman's loveliness, or purest charm
Of unsophisticated Infant grace,—
Where is the eye that is not tearful now?
The magic hand, of nature-gifted pow'r
And cultivated art-accomplish'd skill—

That hand, of the unerring touch, is cold;
And the fall'n graver rusts in hopelessness
Of its lost lov'd employment! Only now
Remains th' imperishable of the past!
The labour of a quarter-century
Has left, for present days and time to come,
A world of infinite varieties,
All equal in the perfectness of each,
From highest born in regal dignity
To basest of indign adversity:
"*Caricatura*" had no part in *him*,
Who firmly emphasis'd, without excess,
The very spirit-truth of *character*.
Whate'er *he* drew,—ev'n to the lowest phase
Of the debas'd in man, disrob'd of grace
By brutalising ignorance and crime,—
Still on th' exemplar rested the impress
Of verity so render'd, that the charm
Of art's perfection, with transparent hue,
O'erlaid the vilest subject's noisomeness,
Was ne'er more sure a pencil for " the line
Of Beauty;" nor for " form, and moving more
Express and admirable;" vagueness none,
Only involving truth in mistiness
That leaves us to " make out " the artist's aim,
And piece up his defections. Clean and clear
As the snow-mountain's peaks 'gainst bluest sky,
Did JOHN LEECH sign " *his* mark." E'en as the pen
Of readiest writer, so his crayon ran
Its purpos'd course of illustrated thought
In picture-caligraph: and, as the muse
Of Cowper honour did to Hogarth's art,*
So may an equal poet honour do
To Hogarth's peer,—John Leech!

G. W.

Portishead, Nov., 1864.

---

* See Cowper's lines on Hogarth's picture of " Morning."

The next scrap illustrates the peculiar humour of Prior Tuck:—

An Epistle consolatory to
R. R. SCANLAN, Esq. (A Lay Brother),*
Alias BARNEY BRIAN, *during his late illness.*

Barney, evil leads to good
(So has sung the Poet);
Illness, rightly understood
Is health—pray do you know it?

Health, "av coorse," of mind, I mean,
Not mere health of body;
The last, compar'd with first, I ween,
Is but a Jack-a-noddy.

Illness, such as yours, my man,
Leads to clear decision:
Many things when sick we scan,
In health elude our vision.

Sickness much the vanity
Of earth's pursuits discloses,
Physicks minds to sanity
By alterative doses.

Sickness, too, is source of health,
Barney; for example,
Suppose yourself in want of pelf,
Now you've means most ample.

Artist wanting, we'll suppose,
An excellent lay figure:
You'd suit him now, *c'est autre chose*
When you are in your vigour.

If to paint a Jew or Turk
A student vastly needed,
A glance at you, and he would work
With zeal not yet exceeded.

---

* See pages 26 and 31 for references to Mr. Scanlan.

Anxious one his new-sown land
To guard from rook or crow,
He'd buy you now in field to stand—
But would not long ago.

Barney, don't be in a fret—
If faithfully I say all,
I'm told you can a summerset
Throw through street door keyhole.

Think what privilege you have
To enter uninvited
Each house, and not, like portly knave,
For burgl'ry be indicted.

Yes, in bulk you are decreas'd,
And my eyes deceive me
If you aren't longer at the least
Three yards or more, believe me.

The gas-man, in a desp'rate plight,
Sadder grows and sadder,
Since you have contracted to light
The lamps without a ladder.

Whilst by your sick couch, my man,
And sitting at your feet,
I almost thought you, Mr. *Scan*,
Another Union Street.

Unshaven, stretch'd upon your bed,
If things, I thought, should go ill,
They'd buy you for the famous head
Of Saracen on Snow Hill.

So rough appear your chin and chops,
Upholsterers declare
'Twould be the making of their shops
To have your shock of hair.

They say, so like the front to back
Your caput now appears,
That Mr. Piper's clipping hack
Nor nose could find nor ears,

And when to him you orders gave
Your head to mow,—or rather,

To hack the stubble, the poor slave
Knew not which side to lather.

A warrant, seal'd with wax and tape,
Has issued out from Stonehouse,
Alleging you have made escape
From some adjacent bone-house.

Nay, worse—some people do opine
You've dealt with Sangrado,
That, though the sun doth brightly shine,
You cast no kind of shadow.

'Tis sad with doctors' tricks to cope,
Their physicking and slashing;
You're thinner than a piece of soap
After a hard week's washing.

But comfort take. I can define
A scheme for riches ample:
Travel in the skeleton line,
And show yourself as sample.

Tuck (the Prior).

February, 1832.

Next follow sundry Blue Friar Canticles having relation to the Conclaves and the B.F. Toasts:—

SONG.

Brothers dear, welcome here
  Votaries of jollity,
Now's the time for revel, rhyme,
  Quip, or quirk, or oddity.

Brothers true, of orders blue,
  Merry as we still may be,
O never yet will we forget
  Our learned owl's sobriety.

Brothers tough—in jovial buff
  While we the cup of mirth shall sip,
Let's vow, thus ever, hand in hand,
  To prove the bond of fellowship!

  Brothers bold, may we hold
   Each to each in woe or weal,
  Strong and clear as Balsam here,
   And firm as hilt to sword of steel.

  Welcome joys: Jolly Boys:
   Never sigh—*chatter-pie.*
  Avaunt, Blue Devils! Hail, Blue Friars!
   Hail! hail! *Benedicite!*
Locke.

SONG—"THE JOLLY BLUE FRIAR."

How gaily the life of a Blue Friar passes
'Midst clinking of cans and jingle of glasses,
He's free from the cot to the palace to roam,
And each spot on earth is the Blue Friar's home.
  Chorus—Before prince or prelate, duke, marquis, or squire,
   O give me the life of a jolly Blue Friar.

If his project it suit, he is grave in a trice,
Confesses the nuns and dispenses advice;
But if for a season he pops on the Owl
The Magpie still gaily chirps under his cowl.
  Chorus—Before prince or prelate, etc.

Whilst for other dull spirits misfortunes are brewing,
He drowns all his cares in a glass of blue ruin;
If fun is at hand he is sure to be in it,
And the rule of his Order's the whim of the minute.
  Chorus—Before prince or prelate, etc.
Tuck.

CANTICLE.

When the jolly Blue Friars in conclave unite,
And sip of their "Balsam" from chalices bright,
To blend "feast of reason" with full "flow of soul,"
Their emblems are present—"The Magpie and Owl."

Should serious matter be on the *tapis*,
They assist its debate with a pinch of "rappee,"
In earnest attention each draws on his cowl,
The Magpie is "chiltern'd," supreme reigns the Owl.

> But should they to wit, mirth, and humour incline,
> They heighten their jests with a flask of old wine,
> In unrestrain'd jollity—Off goes the cowl,
> Up jumps the Magpie, and down goes the Owl."
> Since our Order has cause of its guardians to boast,
> Let us ever remember the following toast—
> " The Birds of all others !   The pride of the fowl,
> The Blue Friars' emblems—the Magpie and Owl."

[The above is the versified form of the second toast by Bacon, and is dated October 21st, 1831.]

END OF PART I.

PART II.

Blue Friar Pleasantries.

Brother Glastonbury (Mr. Edwin Lovell.)

Chronological Retrospect of Blue Friarism.

By Brother Roger.

Transcribed from the original MS. found amongst the other papers relating to the Order.

Dearly beloved Brethren,

It lacks but two days to complete the formidable hiatus of eighteen months between our last and present Conclaves, in which interval, monastically speaking, "we have taken no note of Time but by its loss." The old cormorant, Shakspeare tells us, "hath a wallet at his back wherein he putteth alms for Oblivion." (We have each of us one in front, which we have just applied to the same purpose.) And the undisturbed lethargy in which the Blue Box has been suffered to repose for so long a time had well nigh beguiled me into a notion that the Records of the Order were about to become one of the aforesaid alms, and that I must bid "a long farewell to all my greatness"—the Sacristan's "occupation's gone." But the Precept of His Jolliness has summoned us once more round the Board of Blue Cloth, and I would fain indulge a hope that it will not be deemed a "stale, flat, or unprofitable" task if on the present occasion, "we ravel out our weav'd-up follies," in order that we may "see what we have seen, seeing what we see!" Let us therefore employ our attention for a few moments in taking

A Chronological Retrospect of Blue Friarism.
(No. 1.)

To the month of May, in the ever-memorable year of grace 1829, was awarded the inestimable privilege of witnessing the formation of a joint-stock anti-misery-of-human-life insurance company, known to the initiated as *Brethren of the Order of Blue Friars*, the first Grand Conclave of which Order was convened in the Refectory of Friar Tuck, in the month of *July* then following, at which His Jolliness was unanimously elected as *Prior* of the Order *in perpetuam*, and the other Brethren, Locke, Bacon, and Roger, to the monastic functions of Sub-Prior, Clerke, and Sacristan. Canons were instituted for the guidance and good governance of the Order; four days in the year selected for holding the Grand Quarterly Conclaves; Refectory Items enumerated; Costume arranged (the nether monk only excepted); Pamphlets to be published occasionally for the enlightenment of the prevailing darkness of the age, embellished with lithographic sketches; and Library and Museum determined to be formed [Note: The Salary of the Librarian was omitted to be fixed; wherefore he has remained to this day an unpaid *sinecurist*, on the principle of *no cure*, no pay].

The Second Conclave was held in the month of December following, whereat a Canon was instituted respecting the election of Lay Brethren, and *Aubrey Bizzi* and *Donald Barclay* were admitted *ad eundem*. Monastic Sneezers were presented by Brother Locke, and Blue Corporeal Cinctures by the Sub-Prioress to each of the Brethren, and respectively registered as portions of the monastic paraphernalia.

The remnant of this year comprises a brace of pilgrimages on the part of the Order; one to survey the state of a dilapidated monastery on *Mount Batten*, which ended in a regular "flare-up," and the other in quest of the sublime and beautiful at *Sheepstor* and the lands adjacent, the immediate object of their search not being attained until they were almost too hazy to see anything.

1830.

In this year are recorded four Conclaves, viz., in February, April, August, and October. At the second of which the form of appointment of Lay Brethren was determined on; the ever-glorious Blue Box consecrated as the depository of the Records of the Order; Brother Bacon chapûd as Clerke, and Roger collated as *Clerke* and *Sacristan* by accumulation; after which, the Clerke *phantasmagoricised* for the especial edification of his Brethren, and, as Cowper beautifully says—

> "The *sheeted* spectres on the walls did stalk
> Like washerwomen, far too drunk to talk!"

The appointments of *Capt. N. Lockyer* and *Wm. Lockyer* as "Hap-hazard, out-of-door Blue Friars," bears date the *20th of September in this year*, their election to this dignity, created *pro hac vice*, being consequent on their participation with the Brethren in the pains and perils of an expedition to the Laira Sands, to rout certain cockles and caper longers from their strongholds; in which His Jolliness the Prior well-nigh fell a martyr to his zeal in capturing an infuriated eel, by not heeding the rapid incursion of the tide on his very *untidy* nether extremities. However, he was rescued from his danger through the joint instrumentality of boathooks and shrimping nets; and this expedition, like sundry other expeditions of greater note, ended in smoke!

1831.

The months of April, June, and October claim the Conclaves of this year. At the first of which, *R. R. Scanlon* and *Hugh Barclay* were elected as Lay Brethren of the Order; *Rosaries* from Barcelona were consecrated and indued; and, Bacchus, bless the mark! a flask of champagne and a runlet of claret were formally recognised as orthodox diluents of the all-potent Friars' Balsam.

The last Conclave added *Alexr. Dean Roche* to the list of Lay Brethren, and a Refectorial Chaunt of his own composition to the Blue Box. Moreover, certain *Toasts* were duly arranged as auxiliary absorbents of the Balsam and other like fluids requiring their aid at future Conclaves.

The July of this year witnessed one of those singular triumphs of moral courage over adverse circumstances so invariably exhibited by the Brethren when thrown by cross-grained fate among the breakers of misfortune. The indomitable front which they have ever opposed to unforeseen calamities, whether coming as " single spies or in battalions," was never more signally displayed than in their terraqueous expedition to the unexplored regions of *Shag Beach*. The circumstances of that memorable pilgrimage are engraved on the minds of the Brethren with a pen of adamant, and need no restoring touches from that of their Sacristan.

1832.

We again find three Conclaves in this year—in February, September, and November—the 20th of the said month of September standing out with all the prominence befitting its important claims.

Fill every Brother his Chalice ! To the health of *His*

Portliness the Blue Cardinal, the *Cinque Porte* of the Order (the orthography of this last title, by the way, is doubtful). Which of us is likely ever to forget the ordeal of his inauguration; "the keen encounter of our wits" during his probationary catechism; the ponderosity of his eloquence in gratefully accepting the honour of his dignified office; and the Titanic fury of his fun thereafter, when " he thought it meet to put the antic [or rather, *gig-antic*] disposition on."

But
> " He's gone with his Greek and his Graces,
> His snuff-box, his mouchoirs, his back;
> And tho' absent in Conclave his face is,
> Let's drink to our Cardinal, Mac !"

1853.

Here we are once more with a quatrain of Conclaves —in March, April, October, and November—the first of which records the investment of a portion of the monastic funds in a not peculiarly eligible species of property, viz., the sixteenth share of a ticket in a certain lottery, the proceeds of which, if any such had arisen, would in all probability have compelled the Brethren to undertake a pilgrimage to Glasgow, in order to select and take possession of such cellars, garrets, or other samples of masonic ingenuity as might be deemed an adequate and equitable exchange for the moneys awarded to the fortunate holders of the aforesaid sixteenth. The result was of course, *no go*.

Lay Brother Scanlan perpetrated a sketch of the Brethren sitting in Conclave, which when completed will doubtless be published in the *Isle of Sky*.

The Conclave in October establishes the important facts of T. E. Gosling and Wm. Money having been then and there elected Lay Brethren of the Order, a snuff box *to be* procured for the use of the Cardinal, and the presentation by the Sacristan, to each of the Brethren, of an antique ring, date unknown.

November 23rd.—Be this day aye remembered "in the calendar!" What varied recollections crowd upon us on opening the page of our Records enriched with the Monastic Autograph of our lost Brother, *Prism*! Well may we cry with Juliet—

> "Oh! for a falconer's voice to lure *this*
> Tassel-gentle back again!"

How vivid is the recollection of his sequel to the story, or rather history, of Tom Piper. How inexhaustible the train of characters of *every* phase who would at his bidding "come like shadows, so depart"—Ellenborough, O'Connell, Shiel, Curran, little Stone, the property man, "exceedingly inconvenient" Tomkinson, old Hurst, with his "cock-and-a-bull" story, and the whole galaxy of theatrical stars from Garrick to Joey Munden!

The proceedings of this day are recorded in the Blue Archives as having been consummated at a *special open Conclave*, convened for the purpose of presenting a Diploma of the Order to the great Charles Mathews, under the Monastic title of Brother Prism. Lay Brother Scanlan, together with John Franklin and another, were present under a dispensation from the Prior. The intensely interesting ceremony was performed at *the very table we are now surrounding*, and I need but ask a glance at the picture now before us to recall the basilisk power of his eye during the preliminary address from the Prior. The very atmosphere of this Refectory seems still redolent of the intellectual hilarity and buoyant zest which pervaded every moment of that unexampled evening. Would that his physical had but equalled his intellectual stamina, and that our last toast could now be succeeded by the *health* instead of the *Memory of poor Brother Prism*.

This chronology will be continued at the end of our next *long* vacation.

ROGER.

1840, *March 17th.*

A Chronological Retrospect of Blue Friarism.
(No. 2.)
Concluded for the present.

Dearly beloved Brethren,

We have yet six years of our monastic life unexplored, having brought our retrospective review to the end of 1833. The records of the year 1834 furnish us with four Conclaves—in the months of March, April, August, and December—at the second of which our ornithological emblems appeared in *propriis personis* for the first time, and have ever since offered a partial illustration of our friend Boulter's clerkly reading of the Royal Psalmist's metaphor, "like a pelican in the wilderness or an owl that is in the *dessert*."

The jollities of the third Conclave in this year were agreeably enhanced by the unexpected presence of Sir Thomas Dyke Acland and his sons, and he is recorded as having exhibited during his brief stay with us eminent qualifications for the dignity of B. F.

The last Conclave ordains an alteration in the monastic costume by the omission of its leading feature—doubtless in accordance with the ancient distich—

" Says Aaron to Moses,
' Let's leave off our noses.' "

But the absence of this *prima facial* evidence of a B. F. is ordered to be concealed by blue surplices and cowls.

The 27th of December bore witness to a cœnal assemblage of the Brethren in the upper cell of His Jolliness the Prior, when "Crescit amor *nummi*" was held to be orthodox Latin, so long as any portion of a batch of Natives sent by Brother *Money* remained "unastonished." Moreover, it stands on record that one "William Eastlake" was on that occasion proposed as a Lay Brother of the Order, subject to his qualifications being tested after the manner of B.F.s, of which compliment the aforesaid honourable gentleman is, I believe, in profound ignorance up to the present moment of his and our existence.

The records of the year 1835, it grieves your Sacristan to say, are equally fraught with the sins of omission and commission, the months of January and September only furnishing evidence of Conclaves; the latter of which, though rich in the addition to the Order of our ever-to-be-cherished Brother *Glastonbury*, is indelibly stained with the name of one who has left too foul a blot on our escutcheon to need more than this passing reference. Would that the contents of the *Claret Flagon*, then presented and consecrated, could wash out that "damned spot" from our chronology. But

"When sorrows come, they come not single spies,
But in battalions."

So this blow was only preceded by one as irreparable in its consequences as different in its character—the loss of our dear Brother Prism.

"*Requiescat in pace.*"

Turn we now to a brighter prospect.

1836 restores to us again its proper complement of Conclaves, viz., in April, May, August, and October; the first of which enriched our archives with the counterfeit presentment of poor Prism, framed and glazed, and Brother Locke's interesting MS., " My acquaintance with Mathews." (The Sacristan may perhaps be here excused in regretting that the MS. reminiscences by His Jolliness the Prior are not also added to the Blue Archives, to complete so invaluable a record of our bygone glories.)

At the second Conclave in this year we have the following resolution, as the motion of Brother Bacon:—

" That the recent additions to the monastic costume, viz., the surplices, cowls, etc., should only be indued on such extraordinary occasions as may be determined on hereafter; and that at future Conclaves the Brethren do appear in the dress originally agreed upon, and duly set forth in Canon 4"—strongly evincing the deep-rooted jealousy of the said Bacon's conservative principles, smarting under noses being placed in Schedule A as an infraction of the customs under the *Mosaic* Law, and insisting on their restoration, simply because,

" Says Moses to Aaron,
' 'Tis the *fashion* to wear 'em.' "

At the concluding Conclave in October, arrangements were made for the publication of certain of our papers in *Fraser's Magazine*, under the title of " Blue Friar Pleasantries," and the *sheeted* lustre of some of these *Blue lights* is reported to have caused quite a " flare-up " among the *papy*rotechnic cognoscenti.

His Jolliness the Prior announced the receipt of a missive from His Portliness the Cardinal, inviting the Brethren to meet him in his Hostelrie on the last day of this year on recondite matters of a culinary nature, the discussion of which matters having been unavoidably postponed has ever since formed an excellent exercise for the Brethren in the *cardinal* virtue of patience.

The introduction of an incipient Brother, moreover, is recorded in this Conclave, a scion of the Rogerian stock, under the modest prospective title of Brother *Optimus;* as also the presentation of a venerable relic from the extinct Monastery of the White Friars, rescued from a place where, like King Lear, it had been "mightily a*Bews'd*."

It is not the least remarkable feature of this Conclave that it was the first summoned through the restored ancient precept of the Order.

1837.

The Monastic Establishment on the wane! But two Conclaves again—in March and August—the first recording the confirmed success of the B. F. Pleasantries, and the last the introduction and consecration of the "Blue Friars' Sauce" as an indispensable Refectory item.

The month of November relieved us from the intolerable presence of the backslider before referred to.

1838.

"Something rotten in the state of Denmark." A single Conclave only is on record in this year, viz., in September, and that after an interval of more than twelve months!

"Coming events cast their shadows before," for the chronicles of 1839 are marked "*Nil !*" There is a huge, mysterious chasm in our monastic existence of eighteen months—a yawning gulf, which was only passed with difficulty in the month of March, 1840.

Dearly beloved Brethren, I would ask you, in the words of an eminent barrister, to "*only* consider" the wasted privileges of the Order in this calamitous state of things. Is it *nothing* for the *four* Brethren to have held together, "*per fas et nefas*," for eleven years, and to hold this our Thirtieth Conclave in the *very cell* in which we drew our first existence—our B. F. cradle. so to speak ? Is it *nothing*, amid the " whips and scorns of time," to have "*our* withers still unwrung,' and wear our laurels green as ever—the " observed of all observers"? Is it *nothing* to be arrayed in noses, night caps, and Spanish nuts, and be presided over by an owl and a magpie, and *yet* be the *complimented* and cherished companions of a Mathews and a Macaulay ? Is it *nothing* to have a librarian without a library, and bring the mind to such a chastened state of discipline as readily and contentedly to be turned out of the throne in your own dominions, and cheerfully abdicate in favour of His Jolliness the Prior ? And lastly, Is it *nothing* to have *such* a Prior, and for four days in the year to be Locked and Baconed and Rogered by him to your heart's content ?

Dearly beloved Brethren, desert not these privileges, I implore you, but let's stand up for the Order like bricks, and cement our glorious reunion by an *outdoor* excursion once more to our ever memorable terraqueous property at Shaugh Bridge, and there *mix our liquors* in the unrestrained zest of true Blue Friarship, is the prayer of your Sacristan,

ROGER.

1840, *April* 21st.

A Chronological Retrospect of Blue Friarism.
(No. 3.)

Dearly beloved Brethren,
　　　　The last number of our Retrospective Review was published in March, 1840, and contained the following Records of the Conclave then held. Resolution :—

"Resolved,—that in order to avoid the recurrence of so unprecedented and unpardonable an hiatus between the meetings of the Fraternity as the Records of the Order have this day presented, the Grand Conclaves shall in future be held in Strict Conformity with the fourth Canon of the Order, viz., on the 20th days of the months of January, April, July, and October respectively." The result of that good resolve proves the necessity of an occasional number of the B. F. Retrospective Review as a tonic, whenever our Body exhibits a state of relaxation. *Four* Conclaves were held in that year, in the months of March, April, July, and October. At the first, a new Edition of the Minor Seal of the Order for the especial use of His Jolliness the Prior, to be worn by him on all occasions of Monastic state, was ordered to be procured forthwith; as also a Monastic Snuff Box, duly emblazoned, to be sent to His Portliness the Cardinal. The *immediate* result was "*Box*, et præterea nihil." The ultimate one, of *sus. per col.*, a practical illustration by His Jolliness the Prior, as exhibited by him for the first time at this Conclave. The induing of new Caps and Proboscos, and the presence of Barclay Fox under a suitable dispensation, also stands on the same Record.

The Second Conclave in this year was rendered somewhat remarkable by an aqueous display on the part of the Prior. The refectory table *groaned under* the abundance of the fluid, and so did the *Brethren*, but despite the charms of variety being carried out to the tempting extent of "Bilge, Pump, Ditch, and Soapy," and in the talk of the Fraternity being generally acknowledged to be "*Dry Dogs*," they refused the Water, and only "*whined*."

An unhappy eccentricity attaches to the next Conclave in this year, from the diagonal movements of the bottles throughout the Refection. *Brother Bacon was absent.* As a Geometrician, he was bound to estimate in its full force the exceeding discomfort of a triangle. As a *Brother*, we hope it is a figure he will never again offer for our refectorial solution.

The month of October gave us our fourth Conclave, and the addition of sundry Misses McCullum to our Lay Sisterhood.

Would that the Monastic Records of 1840 had ended here; but the 18th of the following December severed us in this world from one, the joyous simplicity of whose heart, coupled with the gigantic attainments of his mind, has left a feeling of deep and permanent regret with all who possessed the privilege of his intimacy. The death of our Cardinal, John Herricke Macaulay, is still deplored by us, and appears to have inflicted a stunning blow upon the Fraternity throughout the next two years.

The Records of 1841 proclaim one isolated Conclave in the gusty or disgusty month of March, coupled with a melancholy and deplorable infraction of the fifth Canon of our immortal Order. The Refectorial circle was maintained, and a *literary triangle* established. The *bodily* presence of His Jolliness the Prior is alone recorded at this Conclave in the Cerulean Archives. This uncomfortable figure (a sort of three-horned dilemma) may suit the purposes of Freemasons, camp stools, military bands, and Marlborough hats; but what the plague it has to do with the Venerable Order of Blue Friars, unless as a punishment for some of their occasional transgressions, I am unable to define. I take an isosceles triangle to be one of these fellows with the corners rubbed down, but I don't see how that mends the matter, socially considered; and what's more, I don't care.

To the month of May was confided the entire destinies of the Blue Friars for the year 1842. A Conclave was held in the cell of His Jolliness the Prior, remarkable for nothing beyond the presence of two stalwart figures monastically arrayed, whose silence gave consent to sundry opinions and observations from which they might with some justice have dissented, the nature of their cloth being considered.

The calendar of 1843 is enriched with four Blue Days, to wit, three Conclaves, in the months of May, September, and November; that in September exhibiting a precautionary care as to the well-being of the inward man of great moment to the fraternity, in the shape of Refectorial Cards, which, like "coming events," cast their shadows "before" each substance that followed, showing them a fair chance of impartiality from the respective Brethren.

Be the 30th of August, 1843, aye marked Blue in our calendar, inasmuch as it offered the Fraternity an opportunity of seeing their Queen and her Royal Consort within the immediate range of their Monastery (so to speak). It is much to be deplored that the various engagements of Her Majesty and the Prince during their short visit here should have precluded the gratification they would otherwise have experienced in being present at one of our Conclaves, and admitted as Lay Sister and Brother of our imperishable Order.

The year 1844 presents the extraordinary phænomenon of three Conclaves held in the consecutive months of September, October, and November. Surely we must have been bitten by some literary tarantula to have brought out this prodigious activity.

At the *first* of these Conclaves the Refectorial Cards are recorded to have been decorated with illuminations of surpassing excellence. The second is noted for its Refectorial elegance throughout, crowned with the addition of an *Amalthean Horn*, "the likes of which was never seen," as Lord Brougham safely observes. The year received its climax from the Prior, whose special summons for the last Conclave, in the form of a brief, holds a high position among the Monastic Documents preserved in the Blue Box.

I shall conclude the review for the present by the same appeal I made five years since.

1845, *August 5th.*

MY ACQUAINTANCE WITH THE LATE CHARLES MATHEWS.*

IT must have been about the year 1818 that I first beheld the comic master-spirit of his day. He was then separated from me by a dozen rows of grinning heads, one row of iron spikes, five feet of orchestra, and a baize-covered table with two lamps upon it. To speak more plainly, I first saw the late Charles Mathews from the seventh bench in the pit of the late English Opera House, on which occasion he enacted his "Mail Coach Adventures."

I was then a romantic youth of sixteen, devoted to what is termed "the regular drama"; and more than doubting the ability of one individual (however divisible his individuality) to afford amusement in any degree commensurate with what I had before derived from a numerous *dramatis personæ*, including, besides several of our best tragic actors, the delicious O'Neill. In fact, I was rather *taken* to see Mathews, by my father, than impelled by my own wishes; and there was a dignified and condescending sense of *patronage* in my going. It was, at most, a forced payment awarded by candour to custom. Everybody was talking of Mathews, and I strongly suspected they talked nonsense. I went to see how far the world was right, and with the charitable intention of setting it right should it prove wrong. "*I* came, *I* saw, HE conquered!" Had the world refused to

---

* Contributed to *Fraser's Magazine*, March, 1836, by Bro. Locke (Mr. George Wightwick).

acknowledge the comic supremacy of Mathews, I should have "banished" it, as Coriolanus did the "common cry of curs,"—yes, I should have struck up for Mathews and misanthropy.

I have never since my school-days been "home-sick," except in the sense of being sick of home; nor have I felt home less objectionable than when "At Home" with Mathews. This wonderful actor was never more happy than in the title of his performances—"Mr. Mathews at Home." It is true the room in which he received his company was very theatrical in *form*,—otherwise, it was substantially the private drawing-room of the most entertaining gentleman of his age; and had it not been for the spikes in front of the orchestra, the pit must have shaken hands with Charles Mathews, Esq., before it wished him good-night. His performances, indeed, were of so truly social a character, that, but for a reluctance to interrupt the continuous flow of his graphic conversation, we should have been prompted occasionally to ask him a question, to make a comment, or, perhaps (in generous gratitude), to tell him a story in return. In fact, he was not unfrequently spoken to by some one of his *guests;* nor did he manifest any reluctance to reply. "What am I?" exclaimed a gruff fellow, as the actor was, one night, in the character of an astronomer, calling over the constellations, and peeping through a telescope at the gallery,—"The Great Bear!" said Mathews.

To enlarge a little on the *social* character of Mathews' performances. They were so personally directed to the audience, that the latter was rather a participator in than a witness of what was said and done by the "gentleman at the head of the table;" and who, at least, was as far removed from the "company" of a stage as from the "ladies and gentlemen" who form the company in front of it. The actor, in the common sense of the word, is one who throws off his character when he gets beyond the wing, and follows up his "Hear it not, Duncan!" on the part of Macbeth, with a request on his own part for a "pinch of snuff" from the prompter. But it always struck me that Mathews was designedly doing little more *on* the stage than he could help doing *off* it; and my desire to become personally acquainted with him was unrepressed by any fears that intimacy would dissolve the "enchantment of distance." Generally speaking, it is dangerous to seek the *Mr.* positive when we are entranced by the HERO assumptive. The chances are, that the philosophic *Hamlet* of last night may prove, at best, the ordinary gentleman, and possibly the common-place, if not vulgar, fellow of this morning. This danger, it is true, appertains more to tragic than to comic *stars;* and, indeed, it is a question whether the actor of farce and low comedy will not *gain* by personal intimacy as much as the assumers of classic dignity and courtly gentility may lose. Kembles, Youngs, and Macreadys are not pervading in the "starry sphere;" and Roscii, as great at least, perhaps greater, have been seen, whose public and private *acts*, like the opposite poles of a magnet, were respectively distinguished by their attractive and repulsive forces.

But it was evident that Mathews was to be looked *into* as well at *at*. Perplexingly various were the shapes he assumed in the course of any single evening's performance; but, however perfect his successive portraitures, the intervening links of introduction and connection evidenced the intrinsic man. Eccentric he *might* be both in mind and temper; but the genius and the gentleman he certainly *must* be; and though *my* "must" was not quite so absolute as *his*, still it gave a smart impetus to the determination I had formed of some day shaking hands with Charles Mathews. "Sweet are the uses of adversity:" they kept me in the background of society; they denied me all introductory means; and, as I was too delicate for impertinent self-intrusion, they taught me the Christian virtue of patience,— leaving me to clap my hands in the pit for many years before he shook them in the drawing-room.

It was in November, 1833, that Mathews came to Plymouth with his "Comic Annual." Through the medium of a common friend, I obtained the introduction, long coveted, though never avowedly sought. A party of gentlemen were invited to meet him; and soon after they had assembled, an invalid's chair was rolled into the room, bearing within its easy embrace the "half-length" presence of Charles Mathews. It appeared as though his eye had scanned us all before his chair made its stop "in the midst." The rapidly scrutinising quality of his glance was remarkable; it flew about the room like the flitting gleam of a moving sun-lit mirror, and seemed in a few minutes to have afforded him a general idea of the company into which he had fallen. In three seconds we might suppose that the following soliloquy had taken place: "O, here you all are, I see—fifteen of ye—ready to pounce upon me, and to examine what sort of a thing I am when I'm not 'at home.' Melancholy man, that! Wonder what brings him here. Ah—*there's* a man with something in him, *I* can see; and there are the three fellows who led the laugh at my entertainment the other night. If that man's looking his *real* character I'm no actor; and if his companion's no lawyer I'm no judge. Come, I know four out of the fifteen, and the four others I *will* know; first, if it's only to discover why they wear those buttons,—and, secondly, because they have evidently an instinctive right to my affections. Altogether, I see nothing to complain of, though that's no reason I should complain of nothing; so I'll bully the master of the house: *(aloud)* 'Pray, Mr. F——, how much longer are we to wait for dinner?'" His appearance in the chair was occasioned by his then suffering from a disorder in his leg, and he had performed a night or two before; though, during the entertainment, his servant was literally employed in dressing his foot under the table!

Some of the leading wits of the place were present at the dinner party, and they played their cards admirably —that is, they played with one another, and left the actor-guest to be a spectator, until he was fairly prompted to volunteer his *contributions* towards the amusement of the evening. Let me speak proudly for once. What did *we* care for Mr. Mathews? He might have been Mr. Snooks, for us! We were above staring at a lion, being forest-born ourselves. We satirised folly, illustrated character, made "laughter hold both his sides" with our mirth, "ravished hearing" with our harmony, and left the stranger-wit, who might, *by accident*, have fallen among us, to prove or not, as he might please, that he was capable of appreciating, as he might possibly imagine, or of enhancing, as he might vainly suppose, the vast enjoyment, as he must necessarily deem it, of a society so brilliant as our own! To be modest, in turn. If Mathews derived no real pleasure from our efforts, there was the more credit due to him for the exemplary patience with which he endured them. "Well," said he, "it is not always my lot to meet with people who are willing to amuse me; and I can't help saying that I consider my best efforts due, in return. I'll sing you my 'Lord Mayor's Show.'" With this, and several other songs, he most kindly favoured us, as well as with a variety of *enacted* anecdotes, and with a continuous flow of conversation, curiously characteristic of the man, and doubtless far more amusing than he intended it to be. We were struck with the readiness with which he poured forth before a few people, in a private room, what another man of equal power and less heart would have proudly withheld, as only to be duly appreciated by the crammed benches of a public theatre.

A "happy few of us—a band of brothers"—enjoyed the delights of his society at this period for several successive evenings; and it was as many weeks after his departure before our minds settled under the reaction of excitement.

Be the BLUE FRIARS ever in flowing cups freshly remembered, were it for no other reason but that Charles Mathews was one of them; and be it the honest boast of him who writes this sketch, that "he, too, is a Blue Friar!"

On the 22d of November, 1833, the brothers, in full conclave assembled, conferred upon Charles Mathews, Esq., the title, with all rights and privileges thereto appertaining, of a Blue Friar. It was the best compliment they could pay, and it was received as if it had been as great an honour as they could have wished it. In the writings of his appointment he was denominated "the Hogarthian spirit of the age;" and in acknowledging the poor courtesy of his admission into the bonds of Blue-fellowship he included the following words: "But there's one word in this paper which affords me a still increased degree of gratification, because, however flattering the simple compliment of being admitted a B.F., it is still more so to find that the grounds on which that compliment is paid constitute some alleged connexion between my humble name and that of a great artist, whose genius, as it is my country's pride, is my adoration. Thankful as I am to the public at large for its patronage and applause, I can't help saying that I have aimed—occasionally at least—at a loftier fame than has been awarded to me (*I don't* complain—the public has, no doubt, done more for me than I merit,—I'm not talking of my *deserts*, but of my *aims*); and I am therefore peculiarly gratified in having, as far as you are concerned, hit the mark. To have Charles Mathews mentioned in the same page with William Hogarth is quite enough for my ambition; the only damper to my happiness being some doubt as to whether I, the Charles Mathews now speaking, am identical with the Charles Mathews here spoken of, because the names are not perfectly coincident—that is, they're not alike to a T; and, though I have no objection to take two cups of the beverage, still I have no right to more than one T in my name!"

Mathews' few performances during his stay at this period were not altogether so well attended as they deserved to be. The Devonport people were more prompt than the public of Plymouth to testify their enthusiasm; and Mathews declared that, should he again visit the place, he would perform only in the daughter town. To the few, however, who attended at Plymouth he played with marked spirit and care, and concluded his "Comic Annual" with the words,—" And I will say that I never played before a prettier audience, though there are not many of ye!" The Countess of —— was present on this occasion, and enjoyed it heartily. As a testimony that her friendship towards the man was akin to her admiration of the actor-satirist, she waited to shake hands with him when he descended from his rostrum,—one instance among many of the fact before alluded to, that no performer ever went more hand in hand with his audience than Mathews. Being asked what report he should make of his present reception at Plymouth, he answered, that he had experienced in a remarkable degree two distinctive opposites, viz., "hearty, unostentatious, private hospitality, and public neglect: however," said he, "never mind, Gylly;* I came to see *you*, and those friends of yours whom you've now made *mine;* and I should be very sorry if the Plymouth people should think me disrespectful in alluding to their neglect, since I merely state the fact, and believe in there being a cause for it; and, moreover, it's my maxim, that a man who owes everything to the public at large is not justified in finding fault with any particular part of it."

On the last evening of our meeting him in private, he favoured us with his imitations of Curran, and some of our living politicians; also, with his correct and energetic portraits of Talma in *Hamlet*, and Kemble in *Penruddock*. An old-fashioned silver tea-urn was given him to supply the cinerary urn of Hamlet's father: "but pray," said he, "turn away the spout, for that's death to tragedy!"

In alluding to some of his more grotesque personations, he denied the possibility of abstract caricature, asserting that he had seen many realities far exceeding in extravagance anything he had exhibited on the stage; and again, with regard to the laughable effect of many of his imitations, he denied that they had ever involved injury of character, or that he had brought anything into ridicule that was not in itself ridiculous. These are truths of which all who know anything of the world and of Mathews will be convinced. It is not that all people have not the power of illustrating what they may observe, but that many have not the habit of observation. They are so wrapped in their own soliloquial musings, and so satisfied with the limited sphere of their own sympathies, that, when a man like Mathews brings before them an

---

*·His old friend Henry Gyles, Esq.

isolated piece of that world which they have overlooked, they declare it to be an extravagant creation. The isolation may have rendered the fragment more pointedly distinct than when it was harmonised with surrounding agreements and subdued by congenial circumstances of time, &c.; but, otherwise, it *is* precisely as it *was*, and as it will in reality appear to him who can distinguish between *overlooking* and *looking over* the " mingled yarn of life." As to the comic power of Mathews, they who best knew him knew best how incapable he was of directing laughter into any but the most legitimate channels, or of even enforcing his just rights in this particular, when it happened to give unintentional discomfort to any individual. The man who feared Mathews merited his satire; not so the celebrated Curran, who, when he learned that the actor was desirous of getting up an imitation of him, facilitated the means, and purposely enlarged the opportunity.

Our comedian, having left Plymouth, made a successful provincial tour, and subsequently proceeded to America, to remove, by an unreserved exhibition of all that he said of that country in England, one of the most extravagantly false impressions that individual stupidity ever made upon collective wisdom ! It was easy for *one*, in this case, to abuse the understandings of a *thousand*, and AMERICA had been made to believe, by an *American*, that Mr. Mathews had set on his English audiences to laugh at her. It turned out, however, that he had only made us laugh at the *one* booby who had vilified him; and the *thousand* who had been misled now heartily joined in the laugh. It is well known that the actor, on his reappearance in America, was most honourably acquitted; and the courageous integrity which he manifested in throwing himself upon the candour of the people (naturally credulous in regard to their country's dignity) won for him their high respect, where he had before only gained their superficial admiration. But—poor Mathews!—"dearly was his victory bought!" The climate of America proved not so friendly as her people. He set himself right with the latter and came home—to die!

The theatrical public of his country were looking forward to give him a fitting welcome on his return, when it was reported that he was given over as a prey to a mortal illness at Liverpool. He, however, rallied—fancied himself convalescent—and, in the month of May, 1835, arrived by the steamboat, on a visit to J. Franklyn, Esq., of the Royal Victualling Yard, Stonehouse, Plymouth.

I went with my earliest opportunity to visit him. His vigour, physical and mental, as I last beheld it, was fresh in my memory. It had appeared so staminal as almost to defy decay; and it was, in sober truth, wonderful—for though it yielded to death, it never gave up the conquest to disease. I found him sitting upon a sofa, with his arms extended on each side, panting under the distressing effect of a violent paroxysm of hard breathing. He gave me his hand for a moment, muttered a rapid and indistinct "How d'ye do?" then left me unnoticed till the paroxysm had passed. Sad, indeed, was the contrast between the object of my recollection and that which I now contemplated!

But while I regarded him he seemed to get better. His breath became comparatively easier; his face recovered, in a considerable degree, its healthy expression; and he was enabled to speak at some length upon the subject of his suffering on his passage from America ("where," said he, "I passed a *Siberian* winter!"), of his danger, while at Liverpool, and of his having retrograded from convalescence by a measure which he fancied would have advanced him to health. On asking whether he felt any amendment since he had left the steamboat? he replied—

"*Left* the steamboat! What I complain of is, that I can't leave it: it's nothing with me but 'Steward, bring the basin!'—nausea and thirst—thirst and nausea!"

He continued to suffer from the nausea, which he habitually designated "Mr. Steward." It, however, yielded at length before the remedies of his medical friends; but the thirst continued unabated. Mr. —— commiserated him the more from having himself experienced the wretchedness of protracted thirst when a prisoner on board a French frigate; and "where," said he, "having by accident found a bottle of ink, I drank to the bottom." On our expressing the fears we should have of inducing illness by such a "black draught," Mathews for an instant opened all the brilliancy of his eye upon us, and remarked, with as much voice as his then exhausted condition would allow, "Why—all you'd have to do—would be—to swallow—a—piece of blotting paper."

In the midst of his sufferings his unquenchable comedy would often manifest itself; and during the occasional intervals of ease it would show forth almost as energetically as ever. I was more than once surprised by observing that a temporary duration of apparently perfect health would immediately succeed a paroxysm which I had feared would have ended in death. Soon after his arrival, his medical friends deemed it imperative to send for his wife and son. Would that my introduction to such companionship had been under other than such circumstances!

The newspapers at this time were giving publicity to a report that "Mr. Mathews was rapidly gaining strength, and might soon be expected to resume his professional duties." "Oh, very well," said the invalid; "I'm *very* glad I give satisfaction. I'm only sorry that my poor doctors here know nothing about all this, because it is *rather* hard they should have so much trouble with a man who has got nothing the matter with him; and you'll say it is equally obstinate in me to continue occupying your attention. I wish one of you (if you have any interest with the local press) would just help the newsmongers a little. Since *they* say I'm so much better, *you* can say *how* much; and then, perhaps, they'll follow it up by saying when I shall be quite well. They'll also, I hope, while they're about it, inform me where I shall be at the time; because otherwise I shan't know. I fancied, for instance, that I was staying at the Victualling Yard, Stonehouse; but this newspaper tells me I'm still at Liverpool! I *didn't* know it."

He was prohibited from much talking; but when his spirits were up it was as difficult for him to maintain silence as for us to wish him to do so. When suddenly checked by exhaustion or a paroxysm, he would say,— "There, now; you leave *me* to do all the talking, while you all know I ought not to speak. It's quite enough for me to get a word in edgeways. Now *do* talk to one another, there's good boys, and never mind me. Here, H——, are not you and W—— opposed in politics? Say something to hurt his feelings, there's a good fellow: get up a political quarrel—it'll amuse me." We went at it like bull-dogs,—my Tory* opponent fastening on me with the fangs of recrimination, and making me writhe with sarcasm. "Bravo!" said Mathews, as he lay his length upon a sofa; "go on, H——; it's all right: he's

---

* Our correspondent is a Whig; notwithstanding which, we believe perfect reliance may be placed in his statements.—O. Y.

[It must be remembered that *Fraser's* was a Tory Magazine of the most pronounced type.—ED. "Blue Friars."]

getting savage—hear! hear!—à la lanterne! Rascals! Radicals! Robespierre! Keep it up! he's coming to the climax of personal violence. Get some policemen ready, and pray light my bed-candle. Good night—good night; God bless you! and you—and you (then, after a pause, and making a formal bow);—Mr. W——, my compliments to Mrs. W." He could not, however, even carry his *mimic* hostility out of the room, but turned to shake hands with me at the door.

Mathews had his political bias, and his mind was sometimes, during his last illness, distressingly haunted by the conflicting spirits of Whigism and Toryism. I found him one evening sitting on the side of his bed, attentively regarding a pile of pillows which had been placed there to support him in a half-recumbent position. "You'll say it's very ridiculous," said he; "but during the last five minutes I've been maintaining a violent argument with those pillows, which became suddenly transformed into the person of * * * the member for——; and I've worked myself into a fever, because he swears that he won't give up his hateful measure on the—— question. Now what *does* it matter to me? I only wish I could fix my eyes upon something which would give an entirely new direction to my thoughts. As it is, everything I see reminds me of what I want to forget. There's Bulwer's new novel; I *can't* get rid of it. That window looks out upon a quantity of unfinished walling and excavations, which *you* suppose form part of the Victualling Office new works; but to *me* that's Pompeii; and, though you may think that it is old F—— there, walking by a lime-kiln, I say it's Glaucus in the street of tombs."

He several times took leave of his family and friends under the conviction that he was dying. On one of these melancholy occasions I was present. A paroxysm of frightful violence suddenly came on, accompanied with alarming faintness. His fondness as a husband, father, and friend was most affectingly manifested in the sad farewell which he fancied he was then taking; and the condition of his soul was impressively shown by the prayer which, with uplifted hands, he addressed to his Maker. His surgeon alone maintained his composure, and bade us qualify our emotions, under the reasonable expectation of his getting through this, as he had through other fits of equal violence. It was impossible, however, for the unprofessional mind to regard his death-like struggle as less than it seemed to be. The words which he uttered were of too domestic and delicate a nature for publication; neither shall I set down the words of his precatory offering. A preparation of ether was administered to him. Its reviving effect at first prompted him to question the kindness which restores, only for additional suffering, a man who had resigned himself to death. In a few moments, however, gratitude superseded regret; and in a quarter of an hour after he had been at the worst he was as well as at any time during the last months of his life.

He delighted in affording an agreeable surprise to his friends, as the following fact will show. His medical attendants had left him one morning exceedingly ill, and without hope of his leaving his bed for the day. Such was their anxiety that they shortly repeated their visit, and proceeded immediately, as a matter of course, to his bedroom. There he was, to all appearance, lying, as they left him, a little more than his nightcap visible above the bed-clothes. In short, there was nothing beneath them more than a stuffed mockery; for the man himself had arisen, shaved, washed, neatly dressed himself, and walked, unassisted, downstairs into the sitting-room, where he received his surprised visitors with a significant "Aha!"

I called upon him one evening, and took the liberty of introducing a friend. During our stay, several visitors from time to time came in. It struck me that Mathews was more than usually irritable. I caught his eye, and he beckoned me to a close parley. "I don't know whether *you're* aware of it, but I've observed that your friend has given up his seat successively to each new comer since your arrival. He has now occupied for a brief moment every chair in the room—*except* one; and I wish you'd ask him to secure that, and not suffer the next comer to take it from him. It's really hard upon him, because he gets no thanks; and I'm sure he must be tired, if it's only from bobbing up and down. You can't think how it fidgets me. Now, pray ask him to sit down and hold fast."

In the latter end of June he removed from the Victualling Yard to a lodging-house in Lockyer Street, Plymouth, where he was within a short distance from the *Hoe*, so remarkable for its elevated promenade and the noble prospect which it commands. To this charming spot he was several times carried in a wheeled chair; and he would sit watching the numerous vessels sailing in all directions, more particularly looking out for the little pleasure-boat of his friend Mr. Gyles. He had been on three or four occasions disappointed in not seeing it; and thwarted curiosity was (as usual with him) becoming irksome beyond endurance, when positive "articles of agreement" were entered into by the respective parties, that each, at a certain time, should be in a certain express locality. "Now, *is* that Gylly's boat?" said Matthews to Mrs. G. Mrs. G. could not tell. "Humph; well, that *is* odd. Here's a woman don't know her own husband's boat." He, however, espied the boat at last, and watched it with that ever-lively and childlike interest which constituted his success as a sketcher of men and manners. He didn't, like commoner men, "get accustomed" to things. His extractive power was such, that it never admitted the exhaustibility of a subject retained by "a local habitation and a name." The tacks of G.'s boat were with him so many emblems of the shifts of men when the winds of fortune and the tides of circumstance are not directly in their favour; and I have no doubt but that Mathews was one of those speculators who often anticipate from accidental metaphor the nature of moral operations.

I was with him several evenings during his stay in Lockyer Street. "During his stay in Lockyer Street!" How thoughtlessly was that last sentence penned! Where, then, was the spot of his next sojourn? But I anticipate my conclusion. It was not, however, a hopeless thought that he might be yet removed to London a living man. His symptoms were in some respects improved, an amendment chiefly shewing itself in a more regular pulse, and the comparative infrequency of paroxysms. He was one evening enabled to take tea with his friends in full assemblage, and to give continued attention to the admirable song and guitar accompaniment of his accomplished son, in whose native talent and acquired grace he took, as well he might, an honest pride. And here it is impossible not to make a passing comment on the success which has attended Mr. Charles Mathews since his entrance into that profession which conferred celebrity on his father's name, and gained and added respectability from his father's virtues. It is something to be the son of such a man; but it is more to be worthy of the parentage; and it is under the impulse of fond recollection and assured hope that the Countess Rousillon's words are here echoed:—

"Be thou blest, Bertram! and succeed thy father
In manners as in shape!"

Poor Mathews was now becoming daily weaker. Dropsical swellings increased upon him. He ceased to leave the house, and was more confined to his bed: still he suffered much less than on his first arrival; and his medical friend left him at half-past ten on the night of Saturday, the 27th of June, with no increased expectation of an immediate catastrophe. As the clock sounded midnight the sleeping comedian completed his fifty-ninth year. It was now his birthday, the 28th of June. The morning sun might have brought with it gentle congratulation and smiling hope; but it was doomed otherwise. A slight alteration in his breathing seemed to indicate a coming paroxysm. Now, as oftentimes before, it was an immediate summons to his bed-side. Charles Mathews was no more!

He had only lived half an hour into his birthday—a day which, having reason to be proud of the being whom it had ushered into life, claimed the privilege of "lighting him to dusty death." The sad duty of preparing for his funeral devolved on his long-attached friend, Henry Gyles, Esq.; and on Friday morning, the 3rd of July, his remains were consigned to the tomb. All honours that could be offered on the occasion were proudly, not less than feelingly, paid; and such a general sympathy was awakened as really seemed to betoken a national loss. The rank, intellect, and respectability of the three towns of Devonport, Stonehouse, and Plymouth were satisfactorily represented by the pall-bearers and the numerous gentlemen who attended. The officiating clergy of the parish, and the churchwardens, manifested a gentleness of attention which will not be forgotten: the organist accompanied the deceased comedian to the grave with the most solemn tones of sacred harmony; and he was lowered into his tomb amid the heavy sighs and irrepressible tears—not of the *chief* mourner only!

Such was the affecting end of "dear Charles Mathews," as the feeling Coleridge designated him. Had he died in London, friends more numerous, "trappings of woe" more pompous, and a train more theatrical would doubtless have attended on his exit; but nowhere could he have been followed by friends more affectionate, nor waited on by ceremonies more truly suitable and decent than at Plymouth. Even the *day* seemed to take a part in the duties of the occasion. It rained until the mournful procession began to move forward, when it suddenly became dry—still, however, veiling itself from the sun until the return of the mourners from the church, when the clouds were partially dispelled and a gleam of sober cheerfulness admitted.

He lies in a vault in the western vestibule of the fine old church of St. Andrew, at Plymouth. A man so interwoven with the public should lie in such a place interred. Hundreds weekly pass *his* tomb in their way to prepare for that last home to which they are also hastening; and the verger who points out the interesting spot to the stranger, testifies to the words of the pathetic Tristram,—" not a passenger goes by without stopping to cast a look upon it, and sighing, as he walks on,

'Alas! poor Yorick!'"

A brief while longer. I cannot help lingering over his grave—for I knew him as a man—*you*, perhaps, only as an actor. I had opportunities of observing his scrupulous integrity; his affectionate and grateful attachment to those who loved him; and, more than all, his Christian resignation when threatened by the death which has since laid him low. Nor will you, * * *, superciliously smile at my melancholy—for, while from the best motives you are opposed to the theatre (or, rather, let us hope, from the abuses which too frequently degrade it), you will with holy charity take upon report the exalted character of the individual; and though you may never have afforded a smile to his mirth, you will not, surely, hesitate to breathe a sigh over his grave!

And now, adieu for ever! Adieu, Charles Mathews! For the many hours of innocent and instructive amusement thou hast afforded, we proffer our gratitude; for thy purity of mind and unsullied integrity, our admiration; for thy warmth of heart, our love; for thy loss, our deep sorrow!

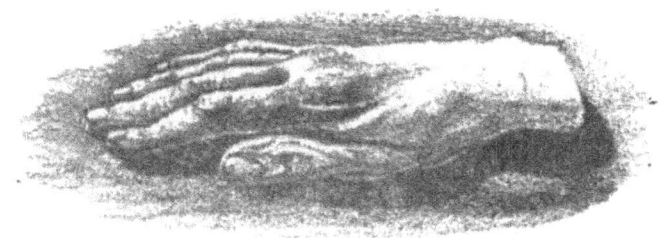

[HAND OF CHARLES MATHEWS.]

CHARLES MATHEWS, in the character of "Sharp," in the "Lying Valet."

PRISMATIC REMINISCENCES.*

By Brother Roger.

———◆———

THE Blue Archives have been this day enriched by Brother Locke in the presentation of his valuable tho' melancholy tribute to the memory of our lamented *Brother Prism*. Shakespeare says :—
> " What we have we prize not to the worth
> Whiles it is ours—but, being lacked and lost,
> Why, then we rack the value."

And this, I think, is more peculiarly the case with the departed sons and daughters of *histrionic* fame.

Hear some Sexagenarian dilate upon the extinct stories of the Kemble and Siddons School; with what a jealous anatomy will his memory dissect every fibre of their Coriolanus and Lady Macbeth, as if "distance" not only "lent enchantment to the view," but also super-added a sense of discrimination not hitherto enjoyed. Every tone and gesture becomes hallowed by time, the play bill of the last century is held a sacred relic, and the shout of Richard, and the shriek of Mrs. Haller, are evoked from its perusal like the voices of the dead.

This novel and brilliant idea beamed upon me some few days since thro' a cloud of venerable dust occasioned by my disturbing the repose of a closet of some dozen years' sanctity, and chancing on a plethoric roll of London play bills, the records of a pretty smart theatrical campaign in the year of grace 1822. I fairly sat me down and fought my battles o'er again. One bill in especial, *like the eye of its author*, pinned me with a basilisk

---

* Read in Conclave, April 12th, 1836.

power. It seemed to annihilate time and space, and throw me back into the English Opera House and the presence of *our dear* Charles Mathews. This bill is indeed *now* become a sacred relic—the well-remembered catalogue of glorious sayings and doings foretold therein came over my mental palate with the full raciness of bygone hours. His " Youthful *Days* " had held many an undisputed sway over my youthful *nights*, and from the vivid distinctness with which some of the characters of this, the *most* celebrated of his entertainments, rose before me, it seemed like a waif on the stream of time, waiting my manorial claim. My anxiety to lose nothing which can be preserved, of the intellectual relics of our glorious Brother Prism, is the only apology I can offer to my brethren for the following *presumptive* evidence in establishing my right to the said waif. And should it prove sufficiently clear to furnish *them* with a tithe of the enjoyment *I* have experienced in collecting it, I am sure of a verdict in my favour. If it is rejected, I can only throw myself on the mercy of the court, and promise not to offend again.

[*On the opposite page we reproduce the original bill of Mr. Mathews' "At Home" Entertainment.*]

The scene of the latter portion of this entertainment, called "Stories," is laid in a lodging house at some watering place; and the eccentricities of its various occupants form the staple of its composition, overlaying a kind of underplot, which turns on the stolen interviews and final elopement of George Tipley and Miss Amelrosa. I shall discard the plot and preserve merely the principal characters—and enter first in most admired disorder Mr. Mark Magnum.

MR. MARK MAGNUM.

" Well, here I am at last, though I should have had the honour of falling over the cliff, and all that sort of thing.

[LAST EIGHT NIGHTS of Mr. MATHEWS's Entertainments previous to his DEPARTURE FOR AMERICA to fulfil an Engagement of long standing, and his Last Appearance in this Country for TWO YEARS.

Mr. MATHEWS
At Home
AT THE
Theatre Royal, English Opera House, Strand,
This Evening, THURSDAY, June 6th, 1822,
(And on MONDAYS, THURSDAYS and SATURDAYS:)
With his annual Lecture on *Character, Manners & Peculiarities*, under the title of

THE YOUTHFUL DAYS
OF
Mr. MATHEWS.

PART FIRST. From *nothing* to the age of *an hour and a quarter*—"First the infant, &c."—Parentage—Childhood—From *One* to *Ten*—"Then the Schoolboy with shining morning face:"—Preparatory Seminary—Merchant Tailors' School—Public Speeches—Latin, Greek, and English—

Song,—"*SCHOOL ORATORS.*"

From *Ten* to *Fifteen*—Bound Apprentice—WILKES, Chamberlain of London—Dramatic Mania of Master Charles Mathews—First attempt as an Actor is *Public*—Fencing—Interview with MACKLIN—The Veteran's opinion of the qualifications of a Tragedian—Elopement from home—Fat Traveller—Ab Llywelyn Ab Llwyd, Esq.——Mineral Waters—Stratford upon Avon—Shakspear's Tomb—

Song,—"*MARKET DAY.*"

Engaged for the Dublin Theatre—Careful Carter—Ingenious Porter—First appearance in Ireland—Splendid Wardrobe—Mr. Mathews ruffled—Old HURST—Cox's Bull—DICKY SUETT's Letter of Recommendation—Hibernian Friends—&c. &c. &c.

Song,—"*AN IRISH RUBBER AT WHIST.*"

PART SECOND. Dublin Company—George Augustus Fipley, or the Line of Beauty—Mr. Trombone—O'Flanagan—*Port arms*——

Song,—"*VOLUNTEER FIELD-DAY AND SHAM FIGHT.*"

Mr. CURRAN (*a portrait*)——Leave Dublin—Real Irish Ballad, "CROOSKEEN LAWN."—How to drive a pig—Leave Ireland—Visit Wales—Mr. Mathews engaged for the York circuit——Interview with

TATE WILKINSON, Esq., the wandering Patentee.

Buckle brushing—Garrick's buckles—Tate's antipathies—Rats—Cross Letters—York Roscius—Overture from London—Mr. Mark Magnum—"All that sort of thing," and "everything in the world"—Arrival in the Metropolis.

Finale,—"*A MUSICAL GOOD-BYE AT YORK.*"

PART THIRD.

STORIES:

In which Mr. Mathews will take STEPS to introduce the following Characters:
NAT—Servant of all-work in a Lodging house.
MONSIEUR ZEPHYR—French Ballet Master—(*first floor*).
GEORGE AUGUSTUS FIPLEY—"A line of beauty"—in love.
AB LLYWELYN AB LLWYD, ESQ.—*not* thin enough.
SIR SHIVERUM SCREWNERVE—Guardian to Amelrosa—(*second floor.*)
MR. MARK MAGNUM—*non compos* lodger—next door.
MISS AMELROSA—in love with Fipley.
The Songs will be accompanied on the Piano Forte, by Mr. E. KNIGHT, who will play favorite Rondos between the parts.

Doors open at Seven.—Performance begins at Eight.—*Places cannot be kept after half-past Eight.*

Boxes 5s.   Pit 3s.   Lower Gallery 2s.   Upper Gallery 1s.

Boxes, Places, and Private Boxes, to be had of Mr. STEVENSON, at the Strand Entrance, from Ten till Five: and at ANDREWS's Library, Bond Street. No Money returned. VIVAT REX! [*Lowndes, Printer, Marquis-Court, Drury-Lane.*]

Lost my hat, and everything in the world. What a glorious thing is a public dinner! feast of reason, and all that, &c.; flow of soul, and everything, &c.; brought away my wand, and all that, &c.; and two odd gloves, and everything, &c. Most happy to apologise if I've done wrong. It's a delicious thing to be steward. There was Sir Roy Poodle, our chairman, I certainly took *rather* a liberty with him. Saw he was getting a little bosky, so I poked my wand in his eye, and all that sort, &c. 'Excuse me,' said I, 'Sir Roy, I didn't mean to hurt you, but I want to prevent you *seeing double*,' and everything, &c. I certainly did *say* some *capital* things in the course of the evening. The gentleman at the head of the table had left the room, and all that sort, &c.; and the stupid waiter placed the removed turbot on his chair, and everything, &c. At that moment my friend, Mr. Blinkley, who is very near-sighted, came in and took his seat *in the dish*. So I said, 'Mr. Blinkley, you're a lucky man.' 'Why, sir?' said he. 'Because,' said I, 'It's well for you that wasn't a sword fish, and all that, &c., or it might have cut thro' your breeches and drawers, and everything, &c.'

There was another capital thing I did. Some gentlemen on the other side of the table took certainly an *unwarrantable* liberty with a gentleman on my right, upon which the gentleman with whom the *unwarrantable* liberty had been taken, seized a decanter and flung it at the head of the gentleman who had taken this *unwarrantable* liberty. Luckily I caught it in its transit, and turning to the gentleman with whom the *unwarrantable* liberty had been taken, I said 'Sir, you'll excuse my stopping the bottle, and all that sort, &c., but you're passing the wine *rather* too freely, and everything, &c.' Gad, how they all laughed. Well, I must get upstairs, and all that, &c., and go to bed, and everything, &c. [*Goes up* the stairs and stops in the middle, laughing to himself.] I certainly did exercise my office of steward capitally. By the bye, I did something devilish good about a leg of mutton. Let me see. Oh! There was a leg of mutton before me, and a gentleman asked me for a slice, and begged I would cut it *saddle* fashion, upon which I said 'You had better have it *bridle* fashion, because you are then sure of getting a *bit* in your mouth.' [Gets up to the first storey and knocks at a door]. ' Betty, open your door, and all that, &c.; I want to come in, and everything, &c.' [A voice from within : ' Entrez, Entrez.'] Hallo, Gad, that's very odd. ' I've made a mistake, and all that, &c. I find I live next door, and everything, &c. I beg ten thousand pardons, Sir, for the liberty I've taken, and hope you'll allow me the honour of calling to-morrow to apologise, &c., Sir,'" [bowing to the door and making apologies.]

There are few characters in which Mathews' *face* played the part so deliciously as in this. As he gave them an account of his stewardship, his countenance literally reeked with hilarious self-gratulation. The recollection of his " good things " made him totter with delight, and were ushered in with that head-shaking throe of smothered ecstasy so perfectly in keeping with his half maudlin state of self-complacency. He was a vinous delicacy, done to a turn. Another glass would have rendered his wand of office a mere walking stick; *now* it shone alternately the emblem of authority, &c., the pencil of the artist, its *real* services as a *necessary support* in occasional inequalities of progression, being concealed with most whimsical solicitude. With what consummate skill was its duty divided in the delivery of a speech which he is supposed to have made in acknowledging the honour of his health being drank as steward! How grandiloquent were its flourishes in eking out the oblivious fragments of his oration, and ever and anon restoring the equilibrium of an incipient totter. Who that has once seen can ever forget its magic evolutions preceding the delivery of the final words, "British Constitution."

Now I must go on to the next scene.

Enter NATTY (a servant-of-all-work in a lodging-house), *brushing a coat.*

"What a pretty set of lodgers we have in this house, to be sure! There's Sir Shiverum Screwnerve—a stingy old hunks—won't afford himself proper victuals for a Christian, that he won't. Says I mustn't brush his coat for fear of wearing off the nap. If he'd been without a nap as long as his coat, he'd be plaguy sleepy by this time, I know. D——e, if a fly was to pitch upon it he'd send his legs right thro' 'em. Ha! Nasty, cruel old devil—keeps his ward locked up in the back of the house, looking at a dead wall all day, because she shan't be married. I wonder she hasn't got a *wall eye*, that's what I do. Ha!

Then there's that great fat Welshman, Mr. Llewellin, come down here to soak himself in the salt sea ocean, as if that would make 'en thinner—an old fool—it only swells 'en up. Always axing me if I don't think he's thinner. Lord bless the man. He'll bust some day, that's what he will.—[*A knock at the door, repeated.*]— Ay, that's right—knock away. The more you knocks, the more I shan't come. Pretty thing, indeed, if a servant is to go at the first knock. I ain't a slave, I suppose.—[*Walks slowly towards the door. Another knock.*]—Well, don't be in such a hurry; I'm coming.— [*Takes in a bandbox and a paper.*]—A dress for Mounseer Seafire. Ay, that's our *French* lodger, the dancing master. Lord, what a man he is—always dancing and talking nonsense.—[*Reads the bill.*]—' A Dress for the *Bal-let*.' Oh! that's a little ball, I suppose. 'Ballet of Cup, Cup-id, -id '—Oh ! I've heard of that chap. ' Cupid and P-s-y-c-h-e,' what the devil's that—I can't make out that. Oh ! I know, ' Physic '—' Cupid and Physic.' I'm blowed if I shouldn't like to see what sort of a dress it is.—[*Turning over the box, and trying to peep in.*]— I've a good mind. Well, suppose I do ? I ain't going to steal anything, I suppose ? Ha ! Can't be hanged for looking at a dress. There's no great harm in that, I should think.—[*Gets the box open.*]—Why, what the devil's this : a wig and a nosegay—and a pair of gauze pantaloons. Pretty coolish wear, I should think, in the winter.—[*Another knock at the door.*]—There's somebody else come plaguing now. There's no peace here.—[*Puts away the dress and goes to the door and takes in a dish.*] Oh ! here's Mounseer Seafire's dinner. The funny stuff he doth live upon, to be sure. This is what he calls his markincrony. I've *often* longed to taste it, and know what it's made of. I suppose there's no crime if I do. My hour's come ; so if I can find a little bit—but it's all so d——d long.—[*Tastes it, and appears puzzled. At length exclaims*]: By Gor ! I've found out what it is— Baccy pipes made easy." [*Exit, with bandbox and dinner.*]

The character of Natty serves little other purpose than as introducing the rest of the *Dramatis Personæ*, and being an accessory in the development of the underplot, viz., the elopement of Amelrosa and George Fipley ; and yet, at this distance of time, it stands prominent in my recollection for as cherishable a delineation of simple individual truth as *our own* "Tom Piper." The struggle between the satisfaction of his curiosity and his conscience, in tasting the Frenchman's maccaroni, was a piece of acting worthy a nobler theme.

Enter Mons. Zephyr (*dressed as Cupid*), *with a Violin.*

"Aha! I am dressed for my Ballet—I shall declare him. Le nom de my Ballet est Cupid et Psyche. Je suis Cupidon—and here are my vings. In de course of my Ballet I shall express vit de force of de Muse, and vit my eye (you look at my eye, if you please) the whole passion of love. I fall in amour vid Psyche, and walk up to her vid grand pace. Comme ça! She no knowing my regard, is little frighten, and retreat from me,—comme ça! I look at her vid my eye (you see my eye), and follow her vid grand pace—she retreat again. I follow her again—she retreat—and I follow—I look at her. At last, perfectly overcome vid de grace and amiableness of my person, she fall into my arms. Comme ça! Monsieur Bull est charmé. He no know how to express his admiration, so he knock his hoof togeder. Aha! I get so much money by my Ballet as shall leave me nothing for de Hops. Aha! Now I shall look at de bill for my Landlord. I am frightful to look at him. For one week's logiment, tree guinea. Bah! It is a grand indisposition upon a foreigner. He might as well stop a man upon de highway, and knock him down with a footpath. 'Tis a grand shame. Ven I live in Londres, in the street of—J'ai oublié le nom—vere all the seven streets run away from one de oder—the Seven Devils—I loge capital for one guinea a week—and den I dine elegant for twopence. A gentleman come every day in his own carosse, fiacre, cabriolet—J'ai oublié le nom—never mind—coach—and he announce his coming vid de cry of cat's me—cat's me—I never could know what dat meat vas—but ver' good meat. Sometimes a leetle tough—and leetle dry—but ex-cell-ent meat—and den so *much* for two pence—I could not eat him all and Pompey too. And dis! Tree guinea! Bah! but I shall go to my Lanlor— if he be great man I shall take de law of him—if he be little man, I shall *kick him!* Aha! Vell,—I must go teach de tree Miss Heavysides to dance. They shall nevair dance so long as dey live: stupid and heavy! But nevair mind. Vive la Bagatelle! I shall see my Landlor, and if he be leetle man I shall blow his nose for him! Aha!!"

[*Exit* MONS. ZEPHYR *in a pirouette.*]

The roars of laughter which always accompanied the distresses of Mons. Zephyr were scarcely exceeded by the tears of sympathy awarded to Mons. Mallet. Indeed these personifications were *idem et alter*—a *real* Frenchman under different phases of character. The sheer truth of *either* stood out in supreme excellence—and the delicate confines of *caricature* were in both preserved unblemished. In Mons. Zephyr the charm was enhanced by the astonishment and delight of the audience at his explanatory interludes on the violin—touched in "the most masterly style." The dying cadence which succeeded his victory over Psyche would not have disgraced Paganini, and proclaimed at once a hybrid descent from Orpheus and Terpsichore.

His next character it seems almost sacrilege to touch —Ap Llewellin ap Lloyd, his fat Welshman. The cuckoo-like question, "Am I thinner, think you?" offered a practical antithesis to "May your shadow never be less." George Cruikshank has preserved him to the life in this character. Each repetition of his query, and the appealing look which accompanied it, begat a proportionate increase of affection for his obesity. With what deplorable accent did he go through his itinerary in search of some deliquescent for his pinguitude—

"Oh, dear! oh, dear! I fear I do not get thinner. I have been to Bagnigge Wells, and Tunbridge Wells, and Sadler's Wells, but I do not find I am thinner; and the other day I was told I must go to the Spring in Martin's Court. So I went there and asked for the Spring, and they brought me a very good-looking gentleman, and I asked him where was the Spring, and he said, 'Sir, I am the Spring, and I shall take the fat out of you'; upon which he put upon my hands a great pair of gouty gloves, and I asked what it was for; upon which he gave me a great blow in my stomach, and knocked me right down upon my clean nankeen pantaloons. Ay, you may laugh, but indeed he did; and I was not a bit thinner. And then he said he was the Spring and I was the Pump, and laughed in my face. I do not know what he meant, but I did not get a bit thinner. Oh, dear! oh, dear!"

The materials of my Bill appear to me inexhaustible; not so, I fear, the patience of my Brethren. I have extracted but a mite from the vast treasury of reminiscences left us by our departed Brother, and added my poor ray to the glorious halo which encircles his memory. Should I in so doing have tarnished his fame, or tired your patience, " my poverty and not my will " is in fault. The flesh is willing, tho' the spirit is weak.

ROGER.

Brother Roger (Mr. Thomas Duncan Newton.)

REMINISCENCES OF LISTON.*

By Brother Roger.

In looking over a number of the *Atlas* newspaper some two or three months since, my eye was caught by a *single word* heading to a short paragraph, a word which has never failed to exert its magic influence over my recollections since the summer of 1812 to this present moment, and the memory of which we would "not willingly let die" without preserving a few fleeting records for the benefit of the future possessors of our Blue Box with its various contents.

What "a pill to purge melancholy" has this six-lettered dissyllable proved to thousands night after night! How many legions of Blue Devils has not its influence dispersed with a fifty harlequin power! What myriads of aching sides have painfully acknowledged the anomalous truth that "laughing is no joke!" And yet, alas, this little word, with all its attendant witchery, is fast gliding into the ranks of the "unused," and will perhaps be marked "obsolete" in the dictionary of the next generation—that, as Shakspeare says—

> "To *have* done, is to hang
> Quite out of fashion, like a rusty mail
> In monumental mockery."

Witness the following paragraph, with its prefatory word :—

"LISTON.

"Talking of paralysis reminds one of the death of Liston. Poor fellow! he had long outlived the active portion of his faculties, and used to stand at his window by Hyde Park Corner, sadly gazing at the tide of human existence which was going by, and which he had

---

* See note at end of article.

once helped to enliven. Liston's "face was his fortune." He was an actor, though truly comic and original, yet of no great variety; and often had credit given him for more humour than he intended, by reason of that irresistible compound of plainness and pretension, of chubbiness and challenge, of born, baggy, desponding heaviness, and the most ineffable airs and graces, which seemed at once to sport with and be superior to the permission which it gave itself to be laughed at. When Liston expressed a peremptory opinion, it was the most incredible thing in the world, it was so refuted by some accompanying glance, gesture, or posture of incompetency. When he smiled, his face simmered all over with a fondness of self-complacency amounting to dotage. Never was there the owning of such a soft impeachment. Liston was aware of his plainness, and allowed himself to turn it to account; but not, I suspect, without a supposed understanding between him and the audience as to the great superiority of his intellectual pretensions; for, like many comedians, he was a grave man underneath his mirth, thought himself qualified to be a tragedian, and did in fact now and then act in tragedy for his benefit, or had done so formerly, with a lamentable sort of respectability that disappointed the laughers. I have seen him act in this way in *Octavian*, in the *Mountaineers*."

My earliest remembrance of him was in 1819, in the character of *Lubin Log* in "Love, Law, and Physic," and poor Yates played *Flexible* in the same farce. Liston's "make-up" of the economic outside traveller, with his various unfathomable wrappers and other preservatives against any sort of severe weather, and *that face* of his peeping from under an antiquated hat fastened *over* the crown and *under* his chin by a yellow handkerchief, which, from its size and colour, might have done duty as a quarantine flag any time for the previous ten years, was a poser to begin with. Then, the anxious scrutiny of the items of his luggage (and what luggage), to see all right; his liberality to the coachman of sixpence between himself and the guard, with the complacent self-satisfaction beaming in his countenance as he pockets the coin returned to him by the scornful Jehu— "It's quite hoptional, you know, my fine fellow."

In June, 1822, "Guy Mannering" was performed for the benefit of William Farren, *he* taking the character of *Meg Merrilies* and Liston that of *Dominie Sampson*. The personation of the latter always appeared to me to be a mistaken conception. Liston's grotesque drollery met only the eccentric irregularities of an unsophisticated and absent mind, without at all revealing the beautiful and indwelling affection which Scott has woven throughout the character. The interview between the Dominie and Meg Merrilies, however, was a performance of no common order, the stern purpose of the *gipsy*, in Farren's hands, contrasting finely with the lumbering and helpless acquiescence of the bewildered *scholar*.

The next play in which these two celebrated performers came into immediate juxtaposition was " The Comedy of Errors," the two Dromios being assigned to them. The affectation of *likeness* between their incongruous faces was the drollest attempt at a hoax ever practised in public. The house was in fits whenever either of them made his appearance.

The farce of " Inkle and Jarico " came out about this time, with a very strong cast—Young as *Inkle*, Liston as *Trudge*, *Wowski* by Miss Stephens, and *Jarico* by Miss M. Tree. The night on which I was present our hero was as full of tricks as a monkey. Independent of the *ad libitum*, and sometimes not very decent " gag " with which he interlarded the dialogue, he kissed Wowski (the only performer, by the way, whom Miss Stephens allowed to *really* kiss her) with such extravagant fervour as to transfer the smut from her lips and face to his own. The effect of the double disclosure on the audience may be imagined. Just after this, Miss Tree came forward to sing Himmel's lovely song, " Jarico to her Lover," *the* treat of the evening, which was most iniquitously nipped in the bud by a grimace of lugubrious expectation which Liston suddenly made at her on the close of the symphony. It was impossible to stand it. She shook visibly, and was compelled to make her exit, assisted by her tormentor, who shortly after returned to the stage, and with the most imperturbable gravity besought the indulgence of the audience for Miss Tree, " who had been taken suddenly ill, and felt quite unequal to go through with the song." The newspapers of the following day gave him a well-merited rebuke for taking this unwarrantable liberty.

Like Farren, Liston would sometimes cover the sock and buskin with the petticoat. Whoever has once seen his *Moll Flaggon* in the "Lord of the Manor," stands as little chance of forgetting it as mixing it with " *baser matter*," if possible. His stalwart and angular figure arrayed in short petticoats, surmounted by a soldier's jacket; his face half shrouded in carroty curls, and a full-frilled Billingsgate cap, whereon was perched a particularly " shocking bad hat," the central ornament of his face being a short well-smoked dhudeen, the which he managed to flirt about in his teeth with all the dexterity of a lady's fan, became a hybrid puzzle which fairly set all conjecture at defiance—how its elements ever got together and harmonised into such a whole. The tornado of laughter that accompanied his strides across the stage, and his look of defiance at the audience as he came on to the footlights, was really terrific.

And is it possible to conceive the chastely dressed and elegant figure of *Bob Acres* on the following evening to be the same person ?

Perhaps a more violent contrast offered itself on the occasion of his benefit, in the course of the same season, when he performed the character of *Sir Bashful Constant* in the comedy of " The Way to Keep Him." Here his costume—a Court dress—was correct and finished to a point of extreme elegance, and his acting scrupulously in keeping with all the requirements of genteel comedy. His very face seemed " subdued to what it worked in, like the dyer's hand," and only once did it interfere with the legitimate course of the drama. In an interview with his friend *Lovemore* (Chas. Kemble) he lets him into a design he has concocted of surprising *Lady Constant* with some handsome and unexpected present. The communication was made with all becoming gravity, but the combined look of present caution and prospective delight which accompanied it was too much for even the stage veteran. He was obliged to walk to the end of the flats and back before he could utter a single word, Liston's face following him all the time with an affectation of stupid wonderment which none but he could assume.

It was on this evening that Mrs. Liston took her leave of the stage, the announcement in the bills being: " Previous to the Farce a Valedictory Address (written by G. Colman, Esq.) will be spoken by Mrs. Liston (being her last appearance on the Stage), *assisted by Mr. Liston*." Being led in by her assistant, she was greeted with an unmistakable warmth of applause which quite overpowered her, and she fairly broke down in a vain attempt to utter the first line of the address. Again was she encouraged by "hands with hearts in them," but she could not rally, and I verily believe the address would have remained unspoken from a sheer inability of utterance, had not Liston, with a *serio-comic* affection perfectly irresistible, taken her round the waist, and administered a series of patronising pats to her head and almost audible chucks under her fat little chin, which had the double effect of setting the house in a roar and herself to rights. The address was well spoken, the points being accompanied by *his* running fire of nods of acquiescence to her, and indescribable winks of communication with the audience. The sting of her final exit was mercifully subdued by the lugubrious benignity with which Liston assisted her off the stage, and when he re-appeared as *Shelty*, in the farce of "The Highland Reel." the house simultaneously broke out into a sort of *double* uproar of applause, as if intending he should take home part of it as a consolation to his distressed little partner. In this character he has to make the announcement " that he was born laughing : the nurse laughed when she took him, his mother laughed as she nursed him, and then his father laughed ; the parson laughed when he christened him, and then the clerk laughed ; and since that time everybody had laughed at him, and he had laughed at everybody."

One had been so much accustomed to laugh *at* Liston in every word, look, or action, and just in the inverse ratio to the increased solemnity of his deportment, that the effect of laughing *with* him never entered into one's calculation. The great delight was to see him in a "fix," "perplexed in the extreme," and watch his grotesque distress and the clumsy and outrageous methods he adopted to flounder out of the toils. To see him happy was to lose half his fun, as we imagined ; but richly did he pay off those who had so deceived themselves and mistaken him. " His great revenge had stomach for them all " this evening.

The delivery of this speech by wicked instalments was decidedly the most merciless proceeding I ever witnessed. He had got you down tied neck and heels, and there he kept you writhing in excruciating fun. The torture became more exquisite at every stage of the disclosure. When "the parson laughed," he began to build his climax. " And then the clerk laughed "—he buried his head in his knees ; and when he arose, and with that matchless face of his literally reeking with agonies of fun at every pore, *gasped* out the *fact*, that "since that time everybody had laughed at him, and he had laughed at everybody," the convulsive struggle for existence was positively awful! It fairly broke through the guard of the most rigid occupants of the boxes, who patiently resigned themselves to the epidemic hysteria, while the pit and gallery rolled about in a helpless state of jolly torment that would require a dozen deep tragedies to assuage.

The mere recollection of it has been quite enough for me just now, and as there is a long career of our hero yet unrecorded, I purpose, with the permission of His Jolliness and the Brethren, to resume the subject at our next Conclave.

In the meantime, any "Listoniana" will be thankfully received and recorded by

ROGER, B. F.*

April 13th, 1846.

---

* This Paper was the last read at the B.F. Conclaves, as chronicled in the Records, consequently these interesting Reminiscences of Liston were never continued.—[ED.]

LAYS IN PRAISE OF SOUP.*

Introductory.

The Brethren were seated in Bacon's refect'ry,
Round esculents choice from their prandial direct'ry:
" The rage of the vulture and love of the *turtle* "
Were blent—like the bump of benev'lence and Thurtell.
His Jolliness, lolling at ease in his chair,
Hath shaken his cowl back, his temples to air;
And blandly he patteth his priorly paunch,
As Burgundy moistens his fourth plate of haunch;
Still more and more waxing prodigiously merry,
He cherisheth fondly a flask of brown sherry;
Alternately cracking his jokes and his walnuts,
And pelting the skulls of the brethren with small nuts:
Until, in the height of this *monk*-ey-ish fun,
His hand is arrested by *Time's*—striking one!
" *Verbum sat*," said he, " *Fratres*; but, ere we disperse,
" Be appris'd, when we *next* meet, we all meet in verse:
" As a poet, we'll find who shines best of the group;
" So let each sing in praise of his favourite soup!
" —A bumper let's have to our next merry meeting:
" One more—then a truce to this drinking and eating."
Out of sight in a trice was each friar's proboscis;
As the last drop is drained, up his finger he tosses:
" *In visceris bonum est !*" gaspeth the prior;
And " *Nil manet intra*," respondeth each friar.
The next time they met, each produced his soup paper:
So judge who cuts best a poetical caper.
Roger, B.F.

---

* From Blue Friar Pleasantries, *Fraser*, January, 1838.

The Origin of Mulligatawny Soup.

Long, long ago, upon a time,
When Hercules was "prime,"
And palpably "bang up" to any freak,
Ancient authorities have said
He took it in his iron head
That he was lamentably low and weak.

And turning to Omphale, his new bride,
Who mused recumbent by his lordly side,
"Omphy," cries he, "pray, tell me what's the work
Proposed for me to-day; for last night's toddy
Has so be-muzz'd my head and floor'd my body,
That, blow me, but I'm at a precious stand
To say what labour I'm to take in hand—
'Tis true, as I'm a Christian, and no Turk."

Replied to him his loving rib,
With ready wit and tongue so glib,
"To-day, dear Hercules, the Bull of Crete,
Of limb so stout, and foot so fleet,
  Be the road flat, or be it hilly,
  You are, dear husby, willy nilly,
  To lug from thence——
Why start you so?—you frighten me.
    Why, bless us!
You'll not of ignorance make pretence?"
"What bull? where? when?—repeat, I say—"
"The Cretan Bull, dear, you're to-day
To drag from Peloponnessus."
"Peloponnessus may be——" "Oh,
Don't answer your Omphale so:
Come, stir yourself, and rouse you from your couch."
And, as she spoke, the patentee of bone,
Muscle, and sinew, drew one stocking on;
And when he'd finished the affair of hose,

This head and chief of all day-lab'rers, chose
(But why or wherefore he disdain'd t' avouch)
'Stead of his own, to don Omphale's clothes.

Now, as this metamorphosis chanced in December,
And Madam Omphy had not, you'll remember,
Another suit wherewith t' adorn her beauty,
She, from sheer spite—certes, no sense of duty—
Resolved, since he'd assumed her toggery,
She'd pay him in his own coin for his roguery;
And as retaliation sweet her soul bewitches,
   Without another thought,
   She search'd, and having got,
She forthwith drew on master's buckskin breeches;
Shoulder'd his club, and donn'd the lion's skin,
Prepar'd for any frisk he should begin.

What light we gain if history we scan!
   We here define
   The very time
When woman, lovely woman, first began
To wear the garments of the nether man:
Omphale shortly after did them doff;
   But some there are
   'Mongst wedded fair,
Who, having once put on,
Will never leave them off.

" What are you for, my man?" his rib asked,
    grinning.
"I'm going," said he, "to try my hand at spinning."
" Sir, your example I'll not be behind in;
   Since that's your will,
   I'll to the mill,
And lend a hand your worship's corn in grinding—
Or, since to change pursuits your honour's course is,
P'rhaps in the stable I shall groom the horses."

Another minute, and this goodly pair,
Professing purposes so rare,
Each for their own route separated;
　　He caring not a copper
　　To say a word to stop her,
Who was, we own, a little jealous pated;
So not to stable or to mill
Went she—truly she'd no will
　　That part to play—
　　So made her way
Back to the work-room door—
He'd entered just before;
Which having reach'd, she ventured,
Sans tap or knock, to open, and entered.

But here appear'd no sign of riot,
Or circumstance to mar her quiet,
Unless the silence that presided
Token of evil past betided;
Be't so or not, Herchy, in dumps profound,
Sat with his goggles fixed upon the ground.

Oft when the human frame has sicken'd,
　　Full many a roving noddy
Has found his right affections quicken'd
　　By a disordered body;
And thus did fancied or unfeigned disease
Work on Professor Hercules;
Whose bullock heart was now much overjoyed,
　　And glad was he within his arms to gather her,
Whom, a short space before,
　　With her caresses cloy'd,
He'd wished on foreign shore,
Where Indian tribe
His spirit might imbibe,
　　And scalp or flay, or tar and feather her.

But this had pass'd, and now they had embrac'd;
And, as he sat, encircling her waist,
She felt his pulse, examined his huge tongue,
   Peep'd down his cavernous mouth into his gullet,
Fear'd there was something wrong,
And hoped he'd try her remedy—
   A liquid preparation from a pullet.
"What! chicken broth? i' faith you must excuse me."
"Nay, dearest Hercules, do not refuse me."
"I must—my manhood cannot to it stoop;
   It jigs not with my wants or wishes;
   For one thing only fit—to wash your dishes."
"Well, then, what say you to some good pea-soup?"
"No,—I had rather be for ever queasy
Than touch that puddle slippery and greasy.
Something provide that will my heart restore,
And make me frisky, as in days of yore;
For now, such nervous feelings me environ,
   That, far from lugging here the Cretan bull,
   May I be crucified if I could pull
A sprat from off a gridiron."
"What say you to potation of ox-tail?"
"Ay, that's the thing,—I'm sure it cannot fail."
"Say but the word, 'tis here at thy command.
   What better to prepare for bumps and knocks
   Than a potation brew'd from tail of ox,
When ox's tail you have to take in hand?"
"No—'twill not do." "Then gravy-soup may chance
Your strength, my dearest husby, to advance."
"No—whilst I live, ne'er shall my stomach's coat feel
   Itself insulted by that hateful mess;
   I'd as soon drink the liquid cooks express

From dirty dishcloths, or black broth of Spartans,
Or that commodity, composed of oatmeal,
  Gulped down by savages in kilts and tartans.
Such common trash might serve for common men,
     But not for *me*;
     I pr'ythee see
  If you yourself aren't able to contrive
  Some rare, some rich, restorative,
To set my muscles on their legs again."

Obedient she, at the proposal flatter'd,
Quickly withdrew, and then her brains she battered
T' invent some rare and precious composition,
Fitting the lion-killer's low condition.
Deep pored she o'er each culinary page
Of every tome that that dull age
Acknowledged to be " crack" in art of cooking;
Solicitous intently did she look in
The Kitchiner, the Glasse, and Oude,
And other manufacturers of food
In early days,
Resolved, if possible, the bays
(Spurr'd to the trial by her spouse)
To strip from their, and place on her own brows.
Nay, she resolved t' outshine the real or fabulous
Art culinareous of Heliogabalus!

The kitchen clock struck one, two, three, four,
And still the matron on her book did pore;
Scullions and potboys her condition pitied;
  Were they alive, they'd one and all declare
They never saw again,
Aught like Omphale's pain—
  Griev'd to their hearts t' observe the studious fair
Apparently by other cooks outwitted.
At length the intricate and tangled chain,

Of various schemes within her puzzled brain,
Unfolded its huge length;
  "Bravo!" she cries, "I have it now;
  I've hit upon the very mess, I vow,
To reinvest my husband with his strength!"

And now was every pot and pan
  Prepared for the potation;
And, soon as might be, was there seen,
Sustained two serving men between,
Of awful size, a vast tureen,
  For Herchy's edification.
He tasted, smack'd his lips, and then
Applauded much—tried it again;
His rib rejoiced to see how he diminished it;
  So quick, indeed,
  His worship's speed,
Ere she could say *Jack Robinson*, he'd finished it.

"Glorious i' faith," cries he, "but rather small
Th' allowance. Omphy, is this all
You've made? If not, pray quickly bring another
  Porringer of that same beverage—
  For ne'er, by Jupiter, at any age,
  Did aught agree so well with me
Since nature's food supplied me by my mother."

In banter Omphy says—"*Now*, art thou sick?"
  "Sick? Nonsense; never better in my life;
  In truth, thou art a jewel of a wife.
I'm better far than well, love—like a brick!
Give me my club again, and lion's skin."
  "For what, my sweet?"
"I'm longing now my labour to begin,
  And bring that beggar of a bull from Crete.
I'll cut his frolics short, and make the beast
Skip here before me double quick, at least.

But, Omphy, ere I go,
I pr'ythee let me know
From thee, my clever girl, the name
Of the invigorating draught, that for this game
Has so well fitted me,
When I had thought
All manhood that I brought
Into the world decidedly had quitted me.
What is it that has made me feel
My iron muscles, and my nerves of steel,
Stiffen'd my sinews, made me stout and brawny?"
" It has no name
As yet to claim;
But, seeing 'tis my own invention,
If you approve, 'tis my intention
To call it *Mulligatawny!*"

Here is another secret, gentle reader—
I gave you one before;
When Omphy, as I stated, at her need, her
Husband's garments wore;
For now (or by our senses we're deceived),
'Tis clear as light, the labours of this son
Of Jupiter had never been achieved,
Had it not been that, rising at the dawn, he
To fit him for the business to be done,
And drive his trade,
His breakfast made
On a vast porringer of *Mulligatawny!*

Then, hail, thou king of every soup, all hail!
Whilst *thou* art to be had
Disown we gravy, pea, or e'en ox-tail,
As puny bantlings of a puny dad;
Oft shall thy savoury steam mount from our board,
Strengthen our bodies, and our spirits cheer,

And, whilst thy renovating steam is pour'd,
  May each B. F. to each be still more dear;
May pure good-humour, every feeling kind,
  Take deeper root, and, as revolves the year,
May we in closer union still appear,—
  Be this the general aim, and we shall find,
Beyond mere bodily sustention,
A higher, nobler invention—
  Mulligatawny for the heart and mind.
TUCK, THE PRIOR.

GRAVY SOUP.

* *Chief Justice.*—There is not a white hair upon your face but should have his effect of gravity.
Falstaff.—His effect of gravy—gravy—gravy.

  Hence, vain diluted broth,
  Of neck of mutton and insipid bread;
  How little you bested,
    Or fill a Blue Friar's maw with all your froth?
With water-gruel reign,
And stomachs weak thy meagre slop possess,
As dull and wholesomeless
As stagnant ditch-water, where tadpoles live,
Or physic which they give
The sickly squad of Esculapius' train.
But, oh, my brethren's praises crave I
For thee—of soups, yclep'd the Gra-vy!
Come thou liquid, juicy, hot,
" Boil thou first i' the charmed pot,"

Then, 'neath cover of tureen
Simmer for a while unseen,
Till grace be said by Prior Tuck,
And thou revealest our pot-luck.

Go, ask our cook the question—"Which in her
Mind is best—or Glasse, or Kitchiner?"
Of all th' Epicurean group
She'll swear the best for gravy soup
Is Dr. K., and then she'll quote him
Thus—I pray, my brethren, note him—

Half a pound of ham in slices;
Cloves and mace the proper spices;
Three pounds of beef quite free from suet;
As much lean veal you'll then add to it:
Then break the bones, or, be it spoken,
Your own will merit to be broken.
Two turnips and two onions skin;
Two carrots scraped and chopped put in;
Two heads of celery fresh as *you* can
Get, then add: and close the stew-pan.
Lest the meat should stick (and burn)
To the stew-pan's bottom—turn:
When the stew-pan's bottom shews
" A nice brown glaze," each cook well knows
'Tis time to throw *hot* water o'er:
When 'twould boil, a half-pint pour
Of water *cold*. Now skim amain:
A half-pint more—and skim again !
Still—still—pour in, as he advises;
And skim—till no more scum arises.
Beside a steady fire then set it;
Gently boil for four hours let it;
Through a napkin clean then drain it;
(Do not squeeze—but softly strain it.)

When 'tis cold remove the fat off:
Decant the soup—and keep the cat off!

The charm's wound up—the liquid's heated;
The prior and his monks are seated.
   Silent, as within a cradle,
     Still the fluid lies:
Off goes the cover—*in* the ladle;
     Lo! what mists arise!
Dimly through the cloud ascending
     Pierce their eager eyes!
Hotly now the soup descending
     Down their gullets flies!
"Oh, how good!" exclaims each brother
     Stifled in his breath:
You hear *one*-half his words; the other
     Scalded is to death.
Mumble—mumble! hobble, gobble!
Turnips—burnlips—juicy—spicy!
Carrots—onions—rump-fed ronions.
   Ever bless the cook!
Oh, she's rich in her
   Learning Kitchiner—
     Ever bless his book!

Gravy soup! thy amber beauty
Claims each friar's love and duty,
Since his heart we symboll'd see
In thy depth's transparency;
And on thy surface mirror'd, he
Views "his effect of *gravi—ty.*"*

                    LOCKE.

OX-TAIL SOUP.

Brothers BACON, LOCKE, and TUCK,
Your Sacristan's in ill luck,
That his first poetic kite
Should be hoisted here to-night:
Seeing that, a week last We'n'sday,
He was racing 'gainst a quinsey,
Winning just by *half a neck*,
And leaving t'other half a wreck.
" Cameleon's dish" and broth of pullet
Were all, for days, that pass'd my gullet;
While leeches added their instruction
How to live, like them, by suction.
Sorry aids are these to climb
Parnassus' hill at any time.
Then let them, brethren, now excuse
The tottering measure of my muse;
And, should the cause of *Ox-tail* droop,
The blame be mine—be yours the soup.

Mulligatawny, Gravy, Pea,
Avaunt! I scorn the whole of ye!
The *first* is most omnig'nous stuff:
Meat of any kind that's tough—
Cheese-rind, nibbled by the mice—
Cupboard scrapings, pepper, rice,
Et cæteras the ear would shock,
All boil'd together in a crock.
In praise of this, TUCK's energetic;
And so am I—as an *emetic*.

Your *Gravy Soup*'s mere workhouse trash,
Vapid, innutritious wash:
An ounce of beef—some bones past picking—
The remnants of a *quondam* chicken,
Scraps of any sort, *ad lib.*,

No matter what, which cook can crib,
Water'd till it can't be thinner:
And, lo! LOCKE's preface to a dinner.

And now for BACON's mess of pottage.
Peas like swan-shot, few know what age—
Parts of any kind of creature
'Reft of life by man or nature—
Celery, onions, leeks, and mint,
Cayenne pepper, without stint:—
Ten hours boil these by your ticker,
And you'll get the noxious liquor
Which, unless I'm much mistaken,
Is so eulogised by Bacon.

Of *Ox-tail* let me champion be,
And you may keep the other three.
"*De gustibus non disputandum*,"
Which means, in my case, "I can't stand 'em."
Then say, cerulean-hooded sinners!
If, at either of our dinners,
Your jaws e'er compass'd such a liquid
As this, which fills them like a thick quid?
So magnetically glutinous,
That your very lips grow mutinous,
And, ere they kiss the spoon a third time,
Are *Siames'd*, like bird and bird-lime!
Potent, ins*inew*ating drink,
Inserting strength in every chink,
And caulking all the cracks and flaws
Made, since breakfast, in your maws.

Eat, drink, and your " quietus make,"
Without the fear of twinge or ache,
With food that scarce shall pass your thorax
Ere you feel like human borax,
And strong enough to match the beast

Whose tail hath furnish'd forth our feast,
To you in soup, to me in rhyme.
But, hark, I hear the prior's chime.
Enough! enough! my paper 's ended—
The least that 's said is soonest mended.
So Mullig'tawny, Gravy, Pea,
Je *soup-çonne* that you're not for me;
Nor shall Bacon's, Tuck's, or Locke's tale
Ever make me cut my *Ox-tail*.
ROGER, B.F.

PEA SOUP.

Argument.—The author of this short poem gracefully setteth out with the subject of his rhyme, viz., Pea Soup. Having duly eulogised it, as holding a pre-eminent station in the Soup family, he very sagaciously doth proceed to treat of the art and mystery of the same—singing of its glorious results—concluding, 'midst thunders of applause, with the triumphant finale, "Britannia rules the waves."

Of all the P.'s in Johnson's Dictionary—
Pe-tard, Pe-ruse, Pe-ruke, Pe-titionary,
Pea-cock, Pe-culiar, Pe-dant, and Pe-nal;
Pe-remptory, Pe-nates, and Pe-tal;
Pe-cuniary, Pe-riph'ry, and Pe-rish;
Pe-rennial, Pe-trescent, and Pe-vish;
The P. I most approve of all the group
Is Pea, the son of Pod, and sire of Soup.
Be't therefore mine to sing, in measured lays,
That soup of soups, Pea Soup's, *supe*rior praise.
Sage was the pilgrim, fearing to refuse
A walk with peas in both his sandall'd shoes;
Who did far more than other sinner durst,

He put the pease in—but he boil'd them first.
Yes, he was wise who thus on priestcraft stole,
And eased at once his body and his *soul:*
Yet wiser he who, scorning so to stoop,
Converted *Pe*-nance into rich Pea Soup.
Say, reverent Genii of the cooking trade,
How may this famous compound best be made?
But, ere the secret thou unfold'st, O Muse!
Give more attention to your P.'s than Q.'s.
The vulgar mode produces pottage merely,—
Split pease and water, bacon looking queerly;
Sagacious cooks, however, do not spare
The tender chicken, nor the timid hare;
Good beef they add, with celery and thyme,
And sundry healthful condiments to rhyme.
If their due mixture you shall well contrive,
Your toil and trouble cannot fail to thrive.
But first the compound mix with peas a lot,
Then to the fire drag the unwilling pot;
Upon a trivet let it simmer slow,
And keep the bubbling just upon the go:
Stir frequently the heaving mass, to keep
Your peas alive; nor let them idly sleep,
Lest 'gainst the iron walls they rest and stick,
And get bedevil'd like a candle wick.
This would, indeed, be fatal to the name
Of goodly soup, and prove a burning shame.
Well boiled the pulpy mass both fine and tender,
Quickly your vegetable adjuncts render.
Next work the whole together well, and strain
Through sieve of tamis, or of muslin plain:
So may your board be graced with soup delicious,
Making all turtle soups appear of *fish*-ous.

This glorious soup, in every varied form,
Is food for British tars amid the storm:
Its wond'rous powers in the British navy
Have caused its foes to bellow out *peccavi*.
Hast never heard the wonderful defeat
Which Gallia's frigate, *Blonde*, did chance to
    meet,
When bearing down on Britain's sloop of war,
The bonny *Spitfire*, close by Lisbon's bar?
If not, I'll tell thee. 'Twas at 4 P.M.
Upon a pea-soup day, which few contemn,
That England's bark, whilst hauling on the
    wind,
Espied the foe some few short leagues behind.
" Up jib, down courses, put the helm a-lee;
Behold the tri-colour waves o'er the sea! "
Thus the bold master bellowed on the deck;
And up the jollies jump the foe to check.
At beat of drum, they muster in a group,
And stand a phalanx—charged with grog and
    soup.
Meantime the Frenchman, borne upon the gale,
To board the *Spitfire* crowds his utmost sail:
Quickly he nears the bark of Britain's isle,
Her brave marines arrayed in rank and file,
In fullest hope to seize an easy prize,
And Gallia's prowess lift unto the skies.
But Neptune, god of England's hope, foresaw
" How France and Frenchmen could be kept
    in awe."
Split peas and grog by chemic power unite,
And urge the jollies to a blasting fight.
Strong gaseous forces animate the whole,
Distend their cheeks, and nerve each inmost
    soul.

Each man an Æolus, ready for a blow,
Sent forth a gale upon the reckless foe,
Which, full impinging on the frigate's sail,
Threw all aback, and held her crew to bail.
Thus, when the Grecian mariners of old
The bags unfurled, which did the winds enfold,
Forth from their caverns rushed the impetuous gales,
And dealt destruction on the yielding sails;
E'en bold Ulysses bent beneath the blast,
And shrunk with terror from each groaning mast.
" Morbleu !" cried Nong-tong-paw : " Ho, there on high,
Man quick the buntlings—let the main tack fly—
Stand by the topsail sheets and halliards all—
Our vessel's side is yielding to the squall :
Down ports—in cannon—cut the weather-rigging,
Or watery graves we here shall soon be digging."
I do not say in English this was prated !
So, pray remember it is all translated.
But all in vain the efforts of the foe,
His staggering ship soon sinks beneath the blow ;
And whilst in British boats the crews are saved,
Britannia laughingly her trident waved :
For such the unequal match in this affray,
That pea-soup only could have won the day.
Pea-soup for ever, then, with sundry staves
Of that blest song, "Britannia rules the waves !"

BACON.

ON KNOCKERS.

I KNOW of no item throughout the whole range of the domestic inventory, from the garret bed to the scraper at the gate, so immediately connected with our feelings as the knocker.

In "the state of man, like to a little kingdom," it appears to be the last link of the chain which connects the Foreign and Home Departments; and I would as lief live in a wigwam as in a Christian domicile, devoid of this appendage. As to your house-bells, I hate them as I do the Devil,—with all respect for Brother Bacon's tintinnabulary preference, I do think they are noisy, unmeaning things—mere sounding brass and tinkling cymbals—*vox et præterea nihil*—like some of their fair namesakes in "real life." As Diggory Duckling says of his fellow-servants, " There's no mispression in them." The very servants appear to hold them in contempt—and your *appeal* seldom gains the ear of their court until ample time has been afforded for *repealing* it. How pitiful is the supplication, " please to ring the bell," contrasted with the sturdy mandate, " knock and ring." (For my own part I always feel a strong inclination to haul 'em out by the roots). Now your knocker is quite another guess sort of thing, and may be occasionally made to " discourse most excellent music." What an infinite variety of tunes are played on this little instrument, the modulations of which being all more or less characteristic of the performers! And to what strange scenes do they sometimes become the symphonies! Perhaps there are scarcely two raps in the course of a week but present some shade of difference—either in time, emphasis, or vigour; and to a connoisseur in knocks, each affords matter of much amusing speculation. Let us try the *single knock*. To a discriminating ear even this is susceptible of many variations. From the timid *tap* of the mendicant, coming for his Monday's sixpence, and bespeaking your favour by its *sotto voce* modesty, to the Saturday night's concentrated *bang* of the tailor's "Mercury," laid on with the accent of a battering-ram—stopping the breach it makes in one's peace, with a pair of *breeches*, and causing a whole volley of good orthodox anathemas to hang fire at the sight of a new coat. And at times, what objects of intense interest do knockers become to the fair sex! every pulsation finding a responsive echo in their breasts, and becoming instruments of pain or pleasure, according to the issues to which they tend. Let us suppose for a moment a case of "coming out." One of Eve's fairest daughters about to be launched in that sea of fashion, an assembly room, her little feet bursting her shoes with impatience to try the steps of Hymen's ladder in a quadrille. Time, 7 P.M. A single knock at the door, of rather an equivocal character. "Ah! my dress come at last!" Enter servant: "A letter for master." "Pshaw! how tiresome! the chair will be here before I'm half dressed." A lapse of five anxious minutes produces another rap—the parlour door is half opened—the rustling of a basket is heard—something is delivered to the servant without comment, and the door closes. The agony of impatience with which the interrogatory, "Well, Jane?" is gasped out, receives but slender alleviation from the passing vision of a brace of strapping loaves which the baker has consigned to the tender embraces of the said Jane. The gratuitous information, "Only the baker, miss," is succeeded by knock the third—and the heart of the fair listener sinks to zero, slap, by the discordant yell of " M-i-l-k !" with which the itinerant vendor of cow's juice makes " the very stones prate of his whereabouts." Here a scene of pretty pouting commences. Schemes are laid for the utter demolition of the plaguey milliner's future prospects, and whole parks of little maledictionary artillery of the feminine gender, are discharged at her devoted head—the consolatory hints of mamma as to the giving up the thoughts of going altogether, being ever and anon relieved by divers raps, equally satisfactory with raps aforesaid. The clock at length striking eight, forms the running accompaniment to a knock characterized by a rather more decided emphasis than its predecessors, and the gruff bass of the chairmen "to know what time they shall come," becomes most dulcet harmony, by forming an unexpected diapason to the high treble of the milliner's orderly, with " Miss So-and-So's dress." By the way, before taking leave of single knocks, there is one of that fraternity which deserves honourable mention at our hands, seeing that it is occasionally ' big' with the fate of Cato and of Rome, and the prelude to some of our most cherished moments of enjoyment. I allude to the ponderous and muffled thump of the *dispenser of playbills*, during the ascendancy of a London Star in our provincial hemisphere. At such times what a racy smack does the intervening substance impart to the otherwise lugubrious " thud " by which the knocker announces the advent of that itinerant functionary—converting it into the light tap of a harlequin's wand, under whose magic influence the brain becomes a stage whereon the " black spirits and white " of the printer's devil do " mingle, mingle, mingle " in most admired disorder.

But hark ! there's the very knock we want: a connecting link between the single and double rap—an undecided something neither in the singular or plural number—a sort of dual rap. This epicene performance belongs almost exclusively to tradespeople, and seems to be the result of a laudable endeavour on their parts to strike a balance between the compromise of their own dignity and the chance of offending that of a customer, by giving a rap and a half—leaving it to be inferred that the knocker had slipped unintentionally from their fingers.

But the Lord preserve us! what's that? It must be either a double-barrelled gun or the *postman*. The electric "bang, bang!" floors one like a blow in the stomach. There is something about the sturdy, John Bull privilege with which this knock in enforced, which gives it a decidedly national character. It carries a sort of devil-may-care, "no trust to-day" impudence in the sound of it, against which there is no appeal. One may as well think of evading the debt of nature as that of the postman. But the cheerful alacrity with which the not particularly modest demands of this worthy are discharged, by all classes of individuals, seems almost the effect of magic. There appears to exist some mysterious sympathy of a diuretic tendency between the knocker and all pocket-flaps within its immediate influence. "Open, Sesame" is the order of the day, and every purse is suddenly afflicted with an incontinence of money. It matters little what the condition of the *knockee*, or whether or not he be "in the giving vein." The knock*er* in this instance invariably imparts a magnetic quality to all mineral substances about one's person bearing the impress typical of our Most Sacred Majesty's illustrious phiz, which is irresistibly acknowledged by the hand in their immediate vicinity.

And here, having taken upon me the championship of

knockers, I would pause for a moment, again to claim for them their due meed of superiority over your house-bells. The double knock of the postman, whether expected or unexpected, is at all times, either from curiosity or anxiety, a sound as welcome as it is palpable, and it would require no great stretch of ingenuity to imagine circumstances under which perhaps no sound which the ear can receive may vie with it in interest or importance.

Among the various relative connections of social life, separated by distance from the respective objects of their affection, when the hope deferred hath made the heart sick, and a letter is the only fountain from which the thirst of tender anxiety can be assuaged, who, in the name of patience, would exchange the throb of delight with which the postman's knock is welcomed, for the complicated and incessant tortures inflicted upon one's nerves by the ruthless din of the house-bell during the whole of that indefinite term of purgatory, "the usual time of delivery"? I might adduce other instances in support of my subject from the very fertile source of the postman's knock,—but "patience avails it no longer." I hope, however, to resume the subject at our next Conclave, when, under a fervent hope that an April temperature will have the effect of bringing one's knockers into a little active service once more, I propose considering the knock plural, and its various ramifications.

ROGER.

1830, *February* 5*th.*

KNOCKERS versus HOUSE BELLS.

IN reference to a certain *Dooric* fragment preserved among the archives of the Order of Blue Friars, purporting to be an unfinished essay on knockers, I perceive there are some twelve moons wasted since I promised my Brethren and myself the conclusion of that erudite performance, which terminated at the double knock. With the permission, therefore, of the Venerable Prior, we will now consider the *knock plural* and its various ramifications.

To a susceptible ear, the knocks of one's own familiar friends, whose visits are supposed to possess every angelic character but that of being few and far between, I hold to carry with them (despite their difference of character) a self-evident autograph as palpable as their handwriting. For my own part, I could with a safe conscience make oath to some dozen and a half of these reports. Foul befall the miscreant who should wilfully forge the considerately gentle *tap-tap-tap* of my surgeon in ordinary—Dr. E. M. 'Tis like the whisper of a knocker. The cautious equality of tone with which the three *taps* (altogether not amounting to the baker's *rap*) are delivered is the certain prologue to the never-varying catechism, "Well, Mary, how's master *to-day*, then?" and "How has he slept *to-night?*" Is anyone inclined to dispute the immeasurable superiority of knockers over house-bells, I take my stand here. In a case of sickness I hold a house-bell to be one of the most infernal machines ever invented for the torment of mankind. You have passed a feverish and sleepless night. The symptoms of your disorder have undergone some material change since the doctor's last visit. Your anxiety to see him again amounts almost to torture. Your very heart-strings seem to have been converted into bell wires, and become positive conductors for an incessant series of electric shocks, which are passed through your brain through the medium of bakers, beggars, milkmen, and match-vendors. You're a lucky man if you escape insanity under this most exquisite affliction. The agony of impatience with which you await the result of each peal is little short of that of a condemned criminal on the morning of his execution, expecting in every passing footfall a reprieve. Contrast with this the refreshing *surge* of comfort which *booms* over your fevered nerves at the considerate development of the doctor's *treble rap*, and I am almost content to leave my case for the decision of a jury of bell-hangers! Again: what an emblem of surpassing melancholy is a knocker muffled! It looks like the corpse of a knocker arrayed in its grave-clothes, more especially should it happen to be one of those smart shining brass appendages of modern invention, which has perchance aforetime resounded joyously to your somewhat impertinent trials of skill. In this case it involuntarily impresses me with the idea of youth come to some untimely end. The unearthly *pluff* tone which it emits makes one shudder like a voice from the tomb. I am bound, in honesty, to confess that there exist samples of the taste of the last generation, which, when arrayed after this guise, do partake of a somewhat ludicrous character, and suggest ideas not precisely in keeping with the misery they are intended to indicate. I allude to those ponderous deformities of former days, which appear to have been fabricated for no earthly purpose but to frighten away visitors and court runaway raps. Indeed, I am convinced in my own mind that the manifest improvement in the physiognomy of the rising generation is in no small degree attributable to the gradual reform which is everywhere taking place in this article. In proof of this I would adduce the comparatively small chance one has in the present day of encountering faces in the street for which you can assign no immediate reason why they should appear abroad without the door to which you have always been accustomed to consider them as appurtenant. On such occasions you are almost tempted to raise your hand for the purpose of rapping, until the illusion is dispelled by discovering the absence of the handle. And here I cannot allow this opportunity to escape without most earnestly imploring all married ladies in certain interesting situations, as they value the personal appearance of their offspring, to forbear from visiting at the domiciles of those friends, the physiognomy of whose knockers is likely to prove an almost infallible recipe for perpetuating the race of Gorgons and Medusas. I hold it a fair subject for a legislative enactment, and would suggest its being introduced as a rider in the new Marriage Acts, under the title of " A Bill for restraining the use of ill-favoured Knockers !" Be it known to all whom it may concern, *I* claim the merit of this idea. " If they will do me any honour,—so ; if not, let them kill the mad Percy themselves !" There is yet another rap of such paramount interest to the sex, that I cannot in justice to them permit it to pass unnoticed. Under what magic influence is the knocker disciplined, that, at uncertain intervals each day, a certain number of reverberations, delivered with a peculiar intonation, shall be sure to find such a response in the pulsations of the hearts of my fair friends, as to enable them to swear most distinctively to the fingers of the operator through a door of any given thickness? Which of the sweet creatures, I ask, would at these moments consent to exchange street *knockers* for the most gorgeous *bell-handle* ever created by man? Did time and patience permit, I could enlarge further on this subject to the tune of half-a-dozen quires of elephant paper—but " this eternal blazon must not be."

It only remains for me at present to implore Brother Bacon to remove a stigma from the Order, of which he is perchance the unwitting cause. I charge him " by the Hand of a Blue Friar" to get a *knocker* (a pair if he likes), and not let the sin be any longer at his door that future generations shall be able to say the Blue Friars were not worth a *rap* apiece. Every Blue Brother has his *belle*: therefore should all the Brethren have *knockers*.

ROGER.

1831, *June* 2.

SOME ACCOUNT OF THE NATURAL AND ARTIFICIAL HISTORY OF CORKS.

―――◆―――

OF the genus oak, though the *Quercus robur* be the most revered by Druids and dockyard-men, the *Quercus suber*, or Cork-tree, has most claims upon the affection of the Blue Friars, as affording means for the perfect safety and good condition of their invaluable Balsam; as faithfully retaining, in salutary durance, the lively spirit of their nectareous treasures; and as generously yielding forth in due time, and in sparkling perfection, their thirst-allaying and soul-satisfying draughts.

But the uses of cork are manifold as the good qualities of Blue Friarism, as will sufficiently appear in the following piece of autobiography, translated from the Corkee into modern English.

"My parent tree was native of a large forest near Oporto; nor was offspring ever more attached to a fond father than I to the ample trunk, which had, for an uninterrupted length of time, thriven within my affectionate embrace, while I grew with its growth and strengthened with its strength. At length, the day for our separation arrived. Twice already had preceding brother-barks been stripped away, one in the fifteenth, the other in the twentieth, year of my parent's age. The twenty-eighth anniversary was now fast approaching, when the forest-proprietor's executioner settled my doom by numerous horizontal incisions, and one perpendicular cleft, of awful extent, from top to bottom. The last was the 'unkindest cut of all:' or, if aught remained to perfect my wretchedness, it was speedily effected by the sub-tyrant's myrmidons, who, with huge staves and merciless violence, continued to belabour me until my several divisions lost all their filial adhesiveness, and rattled about their venerable stem as loosely as 'youthful hose well saved' upon the 'shrunk shank' of 'the sixth age.' Battered yet again and again, I felt my last fond hold give way. Every hope was now gone, every filial tie broken. As whack succeeded whack, my several fragments fell to the ground one by one, leaving my oaken papa as destitute and unsophisticated as King Lear in the tempest. O man! thou monster! is it for thee, then, that the sheep bears his wool, and the venerable forest-tree its bark? It was thus I lamented at the moment, little dreaming of the various uses to which, in my divided and sub-divided condition, I should be thereafter applied. Never had monarch or editor so true a title to the plural unit WE as the riven bark of the denuded *Quercus suber*. We had no idea of the vast contributions made by our severed substance to the comforts and caprice of exorbitant man; and we shall, for the benefit of those who only know us partially, depute the severed fragments of ourself to speak distinctively, each for himself alone."

Fragment I.—"I was the thickest piece of the lot, and included in a large bargain made by a London shopkeeper, who, having *drilled* me after the several peculiar fashions of his trade, enlisted me in the foot service; where it will be acknowledged I was largely employed, when the reader learns that I supplied material for a dozen pair of soles for ladies' shoes; a lump for Mr. Kean's shin in "Richard the Third"; three pair of false calves for dancing-masters' legs; and one entire limb, from the stump of the thigh downwards, for an amputated dandy. Of all my detachments, the latter was the most gratified, feeling prodigious pride in a neat pump and black silk stocking, and occasionally enjoying much mirth in the pangs of its wearer and the discomfiture of some mischief-making urchin, who, aiming to stick a pin or penknife into the peacefully enduring leg of cork, would, by mistake, commit an unintentional act of phlebotomy upon the sensitive limb of flesh. I also contributed to give roundness to the hips of a French dressmaker, and fulness to the bosom of an old maid. My chips were put aside to make Spanish black; and I was also employed in a burnt state, at the Surrey Theatre, to give mustachios to an Italian bandit, and to 'begrime' Othello's face."

Fragment II.—" As No. 1. served chiefly on land, so was *I* principally employed at sea, where I had the mortification of being basely engaged by Jack Ketch to save one of his elect from drowning. The knowledge of his having met his doom on the gallows was, in some measure, a balm to my wounded humanity: for, be it known that the young scoundrel, having first preserved his life and subsequently learnt to swim by my assistance, traitorously sold me to a poor fisherman, who chopped me up into a series of forms about the size of a sixpenny pie, and affixed me to his fishing-net. To be sure, though minced into many morsels, I still enjoyed a life of some variety,—sometimes dancing on the billow; at others, sleeping on a watery bed of glassy stillness; and occasionally basking to dry on the sunny grass. An indiscriminating fish would now and then mistake me for a bait, leaving me in *no* mistake as to the sharpness of his teeth, and subsequently gratifying my thirst for vengeance (to which the salt water possibly contributed) with a view of his active but ineffectual writhings in the toils of the net. Portions of me would, at certain times, partially decay and sever from their holdings, drifting into the open sea or floating shoreward, as the tides might order it. One of them was picked up by an old beach-rambler, who has since permanently and snugly established it in the bung-hole of a beer barrel. Another, less fortunate, was found by a malicious schoolboy, who consigned it to the most arduous of all locomotive services—that of a bandy-ball. This was 'fatigue-duty' with a vengeance! It would be impossible to estimate the interminable length of its combined flights (to and fro, here and there, up and down, in and out), although within the limits of a play-ground not more than one hundred feet square, and within a period of time not exceeding as many minutes. Battered, bruised, and bumped, it was about to fly into pieces, when a lucky hit, too gentle to effect its destruction, but sufficient to propel it over the playground-wall, delicately consigned it to a place of peace and security in the evergreen depths of a quickset hedge."

Fragment III.—" I was the largest of the lot, though suffered to remain unnoticed for a length of time in the dark corner of a cork-cutter's shop in Coventry Street, Piccadilly. At length I was selected for use, and cut up after the brutal fashion of the trade into bottle-stoppers, of various sizes. Each of my severed pieces was then 'sorted,' as they term it; which means, that my component atomies (which had hitherto co-existed inseparable, in wood, warehouse, weal, and woe) were, without any sort of regard for family alliance, mixed up with others who were brothers only in misfortune, crammed into all sorts of bags, and afterwards deposited in the counter-drawers of all sorts of shops. Some found their way into an Italian and pickle warehouse, where they were pummelled into the necks of a variety of squat green bottles, horribly sealed in with melted wax and resin, and doomed for months to endure a close and disgusting contact with liquid mustard, pickled onions, briny olives, and burning capsicums. In some cases there was possibly not much cause for complaint; and, indeed, several of my beloved corkies have reason to remember their enviable condition when on duty in the sally-ports of the cherry-brandy bottles.

"A second batch found their way into another kind of preserve-shop. Oh, the monster, man! Tremble, ye forests of cork; and, though spring be with ye, shake off your leaves as though the autumn's latest blasts were upon ye! Rebel ye, at being yourselves imprisoned as the guardians of incarcerated roots, fruits, and vegetable oils? What think ye of being constrained to the contagious custody of preserved scorpions, pickled tape-worms, and bottled children?

"A third detachment went *en masse* into a druggist's drawer, and came out rapidly (though one by one) to serve in the temporary retention of certain filthy compounds ycleped medicines: nor shall I omit to notice the brutality of the apprentice, who, in tyrannical contempt for the reluctance of freeborn corks to be thrust into narrow-necked phials, and forced into contact with bitter doses and black draughts, would crush them into yielding by biting them round their smaller end, screwing them in, *malgré* their squeaks of anguish, and, finally, with a sort of barbarous triumph, turning their protruding heads downward, and jamming them against the top of the counter. Nor does it end here: for, in all the pride of savage pomp, the bruised sconces of the corks are capped with a piece of red or green paper, while from beneath, a label, bearing inscription 'The Draught,' depends in mock elegance over the shoulder of the phial, like the dangling bob of a barrister's wig.

"A touching incident in the history of one of this batch deserves record. The cork conceived a sympathy towards the liquid confined; the liquid acknowledged a sympathy towards the cork which confined it.

" ' What are you ?' said the cork.

" ' I'm a tonic,' said the liquid.

" ' There must be something in your nature,' said the cork, ' which constitutes an affinity between us. Composed of what, may I ask ?'

" ' Chiefly of bark,' said the liquid.

" ' Bark !' exclaimed the cork, with a sigh ; and much mutual condolence would no doubt have followed, but, at that very moment, poor corky was whisked out of the bottle, and the tonic thrown into the stomach of a convalescent patient.

A fourth batch was transported into certain gloomy catacombs, bearing the name of wine-cellars. Around were several huge tubs, and, on the ground, a vast assemblage of green bottles, of a different form and size to any yet described. Anon came forth a couple of men, who, having filled a number of the bottles with liquid from the tub, proceeded to the conservative process of corking each orifice. ' Mercy,' cried I, ' on my unfortunate corkies,' as they were propelled into their situations by the heavy hands and wooden mallets of the bottlers. It soon appeared, however, that I had wrongly estimated their new situation ; and that the sorrows of abridged friendship, which formed the subject of my remarks a brief while back, was not in the present instance to be so immediately exemplified. The wine-corks, at first, liked it no better than the others ; but, when the bottles were laid prostrate in the bins, emotions of the most agreeable nature were suddenly excited.

" 'Surely,' said the corks, ' we have been acquainted before ?'

" ' Unquestionably,' answered the wine, with a grapy kiss, ' we have.'

"And they were correct: for the native woods of the one, and the vineyards of the other, lay side by side in the vicinity of Oporto. This was, indeed, a happy casualty, as they were fated to remain in close conjunction during many years; and if, as Lord Byron says, 'the worth of a kiss is to be measured by its length,' theirs was a condition of supreme felicity. For years did their mutual enjoyment continue: but centuries even have their terminations, and corks and bottles must have their final divorcement.

"A certain fraternity of jolly brothers transferred the entire stock of which we are now speaking into their own cellars, where, though no vacuum is ever to be found, nothing remains for any length of time. The bottles were marched up in daily dozens into the refectory, successively to have their threefold association (vitreous, vinous, and cortical) dissolved. Forthwith appeared a rubicund member of the fraternity, with a hideous-looking iron instrument, spiral pointed ; the which, by a series of remorseless revolutions, he twisted downwards through the cork, despite the distressing squeaks of its tormented victim, and then, with a determined pull and triumphant pop, burst asunder the ties which had so long existed inviolate. The liquid was then transferred from the green to another bottle, of crystal clearness and classic shape, and the usual post of corks occupied by a stopper of the same vitreous material and elegant workmanship. 'Ay,' quoth I, ''tis just the fashion ! The old friends who have guarded, and the old houses which have sheltered, are thrown by, as unworthy even of a grateful reminiscence.' My darling old bottle was mercilessly condemned to the rack, and the iron which had entered into *my* soul was only withdrawn to penetrate the soul of a brother. But (philosophically to abstain from any reflections on his brutality) can anything equal the unreasonableness, the stupidity, of man? No sooner was the liquid transferred, by means of a glass cup, to the mouth of the master o' the feast, than he exclaimed, 'The devil! Why, this wine is infernally *corked!*' 'Corked!' thinks I to myself, 'and how, in the name of Bacchus, could it have lain five years in a recumbent bottle, with its heels higher than its head, if it had *not* been corked?' But I have since learned the fashions of civilised humanity. The gaoler is criminal in the practice of any affectionate regard towards his prisoner. [Memorandum for wine-merchants: Never trust the custody of port wine to Oporto corks!]

"The fifth batch was purchased by a man in the Strand. An individual of the detachment gives the following brief account of himself:—

"'I was thrust into the orifice of a strangely-shaped light-green bottle, and secured against all chance of escape by ties of twine and twisted wire. Unconscious of any tendency to revel in the expanse of illegitimate liberty, I felt at first much surprised at these extravagant precautions; but soon found reason to suspect that there was a certain subtle devil in the liquid enclosed, which rendered such measures necessary. My honour, therefore, as a custodian, remained unimpeached; but the swelling spirit of liberty *within* the bottle so violently strove with the retentive determination of the bonds *without*, that the torments of my intermediate condition became at length intolerable, and I began to lose all sense of duty in the hope that the bottle might burst into a thousand shivers. Day by day my sufferings increased, till I was at length ordered to the breakfast-table of a pale-looking young gentleman, who, according to the report of scandal, had been carried to bed in a state bordering upon inebriety some seven hours before.

"'It was with joy unspeakable I felt the first symptoms

of returning ease, as he began to untwist my wiry manacles, but could not understand why, in the preparations for letting me free, he should so wink and blink, and bite his lips, and hold back his head, as though every movement which gave comfort to me was productive of agony to himself. The wire was now off; and I immediately felt that, if the string was not instantly removed, it would have to yield to the fearfully augmenting forces within. No sooner had this idea passed my mind, than a penknife was across the tightening twine: a moment more, and the string was severed. I upheaved my long-compressed scalp in ecstasy—I felt myself rising like an emancipated spirit from the bondage of darkness; a portentous *phiz* announced the moment of freedom as at hand, and—bounce!!

* * * * * * * *

When I came to my senses (for I had been most effectually stunned), I heard my young gentleman wondering 'where the deuce the cork had flown to?' Anxious for a little repose, I delighted in his inability to discover my seclusion, and gathered some information as to the nature of my movements on leaving the bottle. It appeared that I went off like a bullet, knocked over an ink-bottle, spoiled the breakfast-cloth, left my mark upon the ceiling, and finally settled in a dark corner behind the bookcase. I need not say, that mine was a case of soda-water.'"

Another fragment was purchased by a certain Izaak Walton, whose mode of treatment differed widely from any yet recorded in this eventful history. "He had me," says one of the victims, "cut into the form of an extremely elongated egg; and, having stuck a goose-quill through my middle lengthways, he gaily decorated me with paint, affixed me to a long line of silk and horse-hair, attached the latter to the extremity of a long stick, and threw me on the surface of a large pond in one of the neighbouring fields. Here I floated pleasantly enough, my lower end being immersed in the water, owing to the gravity of certain leaden shots, and other weighty articles, depending from that part of the line which I supported, in the mid-depths below. Thinks I to myself, 'what gabies these mortals are!' The fellow fixed his eyes upon me in ever-watchful anxiety, and thus remained, with the stick in his hand, for at least a quarter of an hour. I was wondering what benefit could possibly accrue to him or myself from such a dull and monotonous proceeding, when he pulled me out, looked at the mysterious matters which had just been dangling in the waters beneath me, and then threw me in again. Something, however, was now at hand. I became involuntarily agitated; and my manager, at the same moment, assumed a posture of the most earnest promptitude. 'What, in the name of suber,' said I, 'is about to happen?' I bobbed up and down, like a charity-girl on the consecutive appearance of all her lady-patronesses. There was something more than gravity—some aquatic power, at work below me. Once or twice I was drawn for an instant under water, and at each re-ascension discovered my employer maintaining an attitude of ready execution; the rod grasped in both hands—anxiety depicted in each goggle eye—his mouth agape—and the left leg planted before its fellow, in most momentous seeming. Suddenly, after a few more rapid bobs on the surface, I was violently dragged under, and under, and under the waters, until my progress was in a moment arrested, and I flounced out as high into the heavens as I had been just before low in the profound. The next instant found me lying on the grass, covered with a green mantle of slimy duckweed; my manager, who turned out to be what is termed an angler, being employed in disengaging a baited hook from the jaws of a most deluded perch."

The last fragment was purchased by a toy-manufacturer; and it was, perhaps, the happiest batch of the lot. Having been shaped into forms not unlike that of a wine-cork, each piece was handsomely clothed in gilt leather, and decorated with short stiff feathers; "giving my person," says one of them, "no mean resemblance to that of a Carib chief. When purchased from the shop-window, a couple of strange-looking implements were also supplied, and my subsequent employment proved by no means disagreeable." In truth, we can imagine a much less pleasing condition in active life than that of the shuttlecock, when performing its airy evolutions between the battledores of antagonist beauty; and often, by the happy accident of a failing stroke, alighting upon the lip, or nestling into the very bosom of loveliness.

Here I shall stop—as who would not, in such a resting-place?*

LOCKE.

* From Blue Friar Pleasantries, *Fraser*, August, 1837.

ON VARIOUS KINDS OF STICKS,

And the possibility of Sticks not having two ends: being short Abstracts from the MS. Journal of a Logical Divine of the year 1785. With remarks by "Friar Bacon."*

---

1. *Introductory Reflections.*
2. *Classification of Sticks.*
3. *What sort of Sticks may not have two ends.*
4. *Concluding Reflections.*

ALMOST everyone knows, who has ever given the least attention to the most common-place things of life, that sticks play a very important part in our every day affairs. The physician and the divine, the lawyer and the judge, the warrior and the undertaker,— in short, all classes of society, from the Lords of the Treasury down to the servant-maid who kindles a fire, are all more or less dependent on sticks of some kind, in their various occupations. Even the Devil himself has been placed on two sticks for the sake of literary reputation.

Nor are these obligations exclusively confined to the more rational of the creation: the inferior animals, as they are termed, often find sticks equally valuable. The high families of the Crows and Rooks make use of them in abundance; and even vegetable life often clings to the stick for support. It was much after this fashion that a logical-minded graduate of one of the Universities, much devoted to the right use of reason, and to metaphysical abstractions, indulged one evening in some passing, or rather wandering, mental thoughts, on those

---

* Read in Conclave, May 9th, 1843.

various pieces of wood, long or short, coming under the general term sticks. Now this gentleman was not only a philosopher, but he was a divine. He denied the possibility of anything as impossible, and the possibility of an impossible quantity having any definite value, in terms of a possible infinite series. "Sticks," said he, within himself, "are certainly possible physical quantities, and are so far subjects worthy of being reduced to a scientific classification"; and it would be as well, he thought, to generalise them, it being evident that they possessed many distinguishing qualities. He determined to make full inquiry into the subject, and diligently set to work in collecting facts.

The following are some of the first approximations, as he himself set them down in his journal in the year of grace 1785:—

Sticks of the first order, or which beat all others hollow.—Under this head I place drum-sticks, constables' staffs, doctors' canes, mop-sticks, broom-sticks, crab-sticks, the Irish shillaleh, and single-sticks.

Sticks of the second order, or Sticks used in a passive sense.—I place in this order crutches, ships' spars, hop-poles, may-poles, wooden legs, ramrods, and stilts.

Sticks of the third order, derivable from either of the former orders,—being sticks of conversion or diversion, such as sticks for lighting fires, treasury tallys, brimstone matches, rocket-sticks, laths, and such like.

Induction, says Lord Bacon, is the establishment of some general principle common to a multitude or collection of facts. Now the general principle to be deduced as applicable to the various orders of sticks we have just enumerated, is this—and a most important deduction it appeared to our logical divine to be—his eyes glistened with delight as he wrote it down—at least so one would think by the clear, careful way in which the deduction was entered in the journal:—

"In every kind of stick yet known, we find two extremities, either of which may be the beginning of the stick, if compared with the other considered as the end. Consequently there are no sticks which have not two ends—or two beginnings."

This important deduction seems to have been very satisfactory at the time, but on a future page of the journal we find some misgivings on the point. He evidently thought by the laws of metaphysical logic that we might find sticks which had not two ends—that the deduction in a former page was not general. Thus he had omitted the circular hoop, that was clearly a species of stick which had not two ends. Indeed, after all, the end of a stick could not be easily demonstrated, since we could never cut off the end by a knife, saw, mallet and chisel, or any other cutting instrument. For supposing a piece so cut off, it evidently was not the end when cut off, but a piece next the end. It was, he thought, therefore certain that there really might be sticks not having two ends,—but then the ends were of a spiritual, not of a material form,—that a stick, properly speaking, had really only one physical end, which was when it became a *reductio ad absurdum*, and was either decomposed by dry rot or consumed by fire. For aught we knew to the contrary, we might, in turning a stick about its centre, put insensible emanations of woody elements in motion, reaching from the supposed termination of the stick into infinite space,—and might in this way give our bitter enemies a good licking after death, in very distant worlds. Aye, and in such way as would make them feel it, too, by a species of intangible impulses in the atomic constitution of their world of spirits.

So that although sticks not having two ends might be

above, yet they were in no way opposed, to fair logical deduction. Any inquiry, therefore, into the interesting subject of sticks, should necessarily embrace these characteristic distinctions, and not be confined to physical sticks only, upon an hypothesis of two ends. It should be extended further, to metaphysical sticks: that is to say, sticks, the extremities of which were woody emanations, and out of the pale of vision.

These extracts furnish some useful reflections. They shew the amazing powers of logical research in bringing physical impossibilities within the limit of metaphysical comprehension, and so, by familiarizing the mind with things not to be believed upon ordinary evidence, give it the power of digesting anything or everything, be the evidence what it may—a very important fact. In this acceptation, the word evidence changes its character,—it is no longer "*video*, I see," but "*non video*, I do *not* see."

There is, it must be allowed, a great delight to the mind in this sort of pondering—because it has always something before it of a misty character—this the imagination delights to dwell on. It is something, anything, nothing, at pleasure, and is always convertible into a metaphysical reality.*

BACON.

May 9th, 1843.

---

* On reading the title of this paper we looked forward to an enlightenment concerning that peculiar mental condition consequent upon getting "hold of the *wrong* end of the stick," but "the delightful vagueness" of Brother Bacon's termination is too much for us.—[ED.]

LUBIN'S LOG.*

"The Sea—the Sea! the open Sea!"
BARRY CORNWALL.

EIGHT o'clock in the morning. Blue sky and bright sun, with a few such silver clouds as a painter would desire. Resolved, after much consideration, to speculate on the continuance of fine weather, and to effect my intended journey from Plymouth to Falmouth by the *Francis Drake* steamer.

12 o'clock. Went on board: ascending the vessel's side with all the alacrity of a practised tar, and strutting along the deck with the steady step and buoyant assurance of an admiral. Unexpectedly met with two or three of my prettiest female acquaintances, who reclined under an awning on either side of the deck like so many Cleopatras. I resolved to exhibit myself throughout the voyage as the very model of a courtly gallant.

$12\frac{1}{2}$ p.m. Impatience relieved; anchor weighed; paddles in motion; our *own* motion scarcely perceptible. "Most fortunate in the day, madam: permit me to take off your shawl": with a continuous flow of small talk most delectable—not *ad infinitum*, but to the Breakwater —and no further.

1 p.m. Our bowsprit, which till now had maintained a tolerably right onward, straight forward, horizontality of progression, became, on a sudden, very inconveniently capricious in its movements—now threatening to poke a hole in the waving pattern of the indigo carpet below us —now aiming, with uplifted impudence, at the mottled

---

* From Blue Friar Pleasantries, *Fraser*, August, 1837.

ceiling above—and, anon, giving its point a segmental sweep from Penlee Point on the west to the Mewstone on the east, just as the leg of a pair of compasses all in a moment steps over Mercator's map of the world from Cape Horn to the Cape of Good Hope. "Bless me!" said one of my fair companions: "I am afraid it's going to be rough!"

The idea of old Neptune being rude to a young lady! To be sure, all that we know of him confirms him to have been a *Giovanni* of the first water—for he broke through the vestal vows of Amphitrite, changed Theophane into a lady-sheep, and himself into a sir-sheep; and, as Ceres chose to transform *her*self into a mare, to avoid Neptune's importunities, why the god had no chance but to change himself into a *lord*-mare for the sweet sake of legitimising that alliance, which (I need not say) led to the birth of the sea-horse, Arion : thence steamboats. Since, however, Brother Bacon may dilate upon boilers and pistons, every man of common-sense is well aware, that in each paddle-box is incarcerated an Arion, who, instigated by the torment of scalding water, keeps continually galloping over the paddles like a squirrel in a revolving cage, and, in his untired efforts to get out, causes the steamboat with never-ceasing velocity to move on. And thus, to return to old Neptune. My fair friend had some reason to fear his roughness. When perfectly sober, he is admitted by the most delicate damsels as pleasant and companionable ; but, when he's "*half* seas over," odds mops and buckets! it's *all* over with most of us.

2 p.m. Gallantry beginning to wax faint ; garrulity changing to meditation ; smiles got up with difficulty resolve themselves into unavoidable yawns: and, look! of the ten gentlemen, who, ere now, paced the deck in lines as parallel and direct as the boards which compose

it, only a tithe remains, the vicar of Rockingale, who, having served a long chaplaincy in the Bay of Biscay, stands up to the last the champion of the Church, and maintains, unprostrated, "the divinity that stirs within him." Certes, the divinity of man and the angelicism of woman, never so decidedly evanesce, as when the sea-god employs them in a game of "pitch and toss." Behold them! All, save the vicar of Rockingale, not only *pale*-faced under sickness, but *shame*-faced under the sense of it. And here, indeed, is the distinctive misery of the case. Be very ill—exceedingly unwell—not at all well—or, simply, indisposed, on *shore*, and you are greeted with pitying sorrow and sympathising solicitude; but be sick at *sea*, and look for no participator in your sufferings beyond the bucket under your nose. And, to many, even the bucket is denied. Behold them, hanging their chins over the gunnel-edge, like so many culprits doomed to the block; and, sooth, if their heads *were* chopped off, their bodies, just now, would be all the better for it.

3 p.m. Discovered the steward to be an impudent fellow, and resolved, under certain restrictions, to "hate him everlastingly," for comparing my face to my nankeen trousers. But, hold! where was my gallantry? Observed the prettiest and most delicate of my lady companions staggering like an inebriated "siren of Billingsgate" to reach the cabin-stairs; yet aided her not! Instead of rushing to assist, I sat on the top of the cabin skylight, staring at her after the monumental fashion of Ugolino.

" Pray, captain, *when* shall we arrive at Falmouth?"

"We *have* done it, often, in five hours."

Now, I perceived this was an evasion; but it was kindly meant: so I took a liking to Captain Nichols. I had not, however, the courage to ask him any further questions—for at that instant, a volley of smoke was blown down upon us from the funnel, signifying that the wind was slap in our teeth. I therefore comforted myself in the assurance, that we were at least *some* way on our journey, and so far nearer its end.

Scarcely had I reflected on the horrors of a directly hostile wind, when the captain (who had been for some time ogling the black horizon with unaccountable pertinacity) yelled out some jargon to the helmsman, and the wind was all on a sudden directly behind us; by which you are to understand, my most pitying Brothers Blue, that the captain had perceived the object of his look-out; and, instead of continuing our proper course, due west, for Falmouth, we made a " right-about" of it, and were now running due east, to meet the *Brunswick* steamer, bound for Plymouth from Portsmouth! The *Brunswick* had passengers to transfer ; and we were doomed, as if we had been so much senseless luggage, without even the faculty of disgust, to retrace and re-retrace our trackless path, enduring the addition of one and a half hours' misery to wretchedness already infinite !

3½ p.m. Came up with the *Brunswick* ; and there were the steamers curtseying around each other, like two black monsters dancing a minuet. "Stop her!" was the word given on both decks ; and anon was heard the deafening guttural of the safety-pipes, as if the Devil and all his imps were simultaneously engaged in gargling their sore throats. Then came a boat full of damp, uncomfortable voyagers, all sickness and shiver, who, after being bruised into mummies by their own luggage, and promiscuously assaulted by boat-hooks, were hauled, through an atmosphere of saline pickle, on to the deck of the *Drake*.

I could keep no longer any account of time. "On horror's head did horrors accumulate!" We turned once more round upon the wind, which beat in our faces a thick, tepid rain, surcharged with the heat of the steam, the black of the smoke, cabbage-water from the cook's closet, and effluviæ varied and unmentionable. "O," cried I, "for a place on the loftiest and bleakest summit of Dartmoor, with a tenfold tempest 'laying it thick' on my houseless head! How fondly would I embrace its immovable granite, and exclaim, 'Blow, winds, and crack your cheeks! Rage! blow!' King Lear," said I, "be hanged. I pity him not. He was never on board a steam-boat. I believe no more in *terra firma* woes: they are mere romance,—very grand, and very endurable. It was all mighty fine for Queen Constance to squat herself down on the green grass, and to say,—

'Here I and sorrow sit—bid kings come bow to me!'

Had it been attempted on the deck of the *Drake*, she and sorrow would have speedily found, that when sea and sickness are among the *dramatis personæ*, they tumble tragic dignity head over heels, and exemplify that *acme* of intoxication which is supposed to be attained when a man can't lie without holding. The settled quiet of a sublime despair would be positively jocose compared with this."

And there was the vicar of Rockingale all this time, keeping his eyes as level as the compass-card, and his body as erect and true to the centre of gravity as the hanging lamp in the cabin. With a white mackintosh over his shoulders, he continued to pace cheerfully to and fro, merely remarking, with exquisite simplicity, that the weather was certainly not so fine as it might have been, and leaving us to conclude that it might have been much worse, and its victims (if possible) worse still, without either his bile or his sympathies being in the least degree excited. That which made *our* faces as pale as parsnips seemed only to refresh *his*. The

o

wind blew additional redness into his cheeks, and the rain varnished them. Whether he had ever been tarred and feathered I know not; but it is certain that no duck ever felt more at home with a drake than his reverence with her ladyship the *Sir Francis*. I know not what hour it was; but, in an agony of qualm, I resolved on "going below." It was a resolution demanding no small effort,—for most uncertain was the speculation whether I should reach my berth in safety, or even with decency. How the speculation answered will appear in the fact of my lurching into the lap of an antiquated spinster, after I had grasped the bony ball of her knee instead of the brass knob of the stairs at which I had aimed. She screamed like a "wild sea-mew," and hurled me from her with a force that not only carried me to the desired staircase (which otherwise I might not have reached), but also afforded the ungentle service of tumbling me half way down, to the manifest disadvantage of a glass of brandy-and-water, which the steward was at that instant bringing up. The noise of my fall seemed to have awakened the dead,—for, on looking into the cabin, I saw what might reasonably be called a corridor of catacombs, with two tiers of suddenly animated "bodies" on each side. It was as if I had been plunged by the dire action of an earthquake into the "tomb of all the Capulets," without even time for a civil—"hope I don't intrude." Such a set of ghastly editions of the human face divine never frighted nature from herself. My gorge rose at the spectacle, and I rushed upwards to regain the deck. A vacant seat near the helmsman invited me; I threw myself along it, and lay extended on my back, blessed in the discovery, that in this position sickness was relieved. Exhaustion befriended me, and I fell asleep.

$9\frac{1}{2}$ p.m. The dazzling brightness of the St. Mawes lighthouse at length awoke me. We were entering Falmouth harbour. I lifted my head in an ecstasy of joy; but a qualm came instantly over me, and "as you were" was the word. Ten minutes more, and the water was smooth. I arose; and, having passed through another ten minutes of intense cold, mingled with eager hope, I scrambled into a boat, which delivered me on the quay, and left me to pursue my joyful way to the hotel.

Where were the fair damsels whom in the morning I had resolved to fascinate with my attentions? Alas! it was now too late to think. While on deck, I cared not. An overwhelming selfishness had wholly swayed me; and I could have thrown them on either side, like so many trifling objections, so that I could but effect a clear and speedy way out of that detestable sea-omnibus.

Delicious was the cup of Bohea, and the sight of the chambermaid, in lieu of that web-footed, lollopping stewardess. Yet was my happiness far from perfect—for the room in which I sate, though stationary I *believe*, was far from seeming so. Still did my habituated senses respond to the burden—

> "See—saw—
> Margery—Daw—
> Sold her bed—
> And lay in the straw."

And, to conclude, if Margery's bed had been located in a steam-cabin, she was perfectly justified in selling it—for there is not a dust-hole on land which, as a bed of repose, is not delicious luxury, when compared with a berth in the rumbling abdomen of that most Satanic of sea-monsters ycleped a steam-ship.

Barry Cornwall's song of "The Sea!" is well known; and it is curious to observe how the most anti-marine lungs have been exercised in recommending it to public favour. Nay, I used to sing it myself, until I learned how to appreciate it on board the *Drake;* since when I sing as follows:—

  The Sea! the Sea! Oh me! oh me!
  The pail—be quick! I quail—I'm sick—
   I'm sick as I can be:
I cannot sit, I cannot stand;
I prithee, steward, lend a hand.
  To my cabin I'll go—to my berth will I hie,
   And like a cradled infant lie.
I'm on the sea—I'm on the sea!
I am where I would never be;
  With the smoke above, and the steam below,
   And sickness wheresoe'er I go:
If a storm should come, no matter, I wot;
To the bottom I'd go—as soon as not.

  I love, oh! how I love to ride
  In a neat post-chaise, with a couple of bays,
   And a pretty girl by my side:
But, oh! to swing amidst fire and foam,
And be steamed like a mealy potato at home;
  And to feel that no soul cares more for your woe
  Than the paddles that clatter as onward they go.
The ocean's wave I ne'er moved o'er,
But I loved my donkey more and more,
  And homeward flew to her bony back,
  Like a truant boy or a sandman's sack;
And a mother she was, and is, to me;
For I was—an ass—to go to sea!

  The fields were green, and blue the morn,
And still as a mouse the little house
  Where I—where I was born;
And my father whistled, my mother smiled,
While my donkey bray'd in accents mild;
  Nor ever was heard such an outcry of joy
  As welcomed to life the beautiful boy!
I have lived, since then, in calm and strife,
With my peaceable donkey and termagant wife;
  With a spur for the one, and a whip for the other;
  Yet ne'er have wish'd to change with another:
And a proverb of old will apply well to me,—
"Who is born to be hang'd will not die in the sea!"
         LOCKE.

POPPING THE QUESTION, ACCORDING TO MODERN EXPERIENCE.*

"POPPING the question!" There can be no doubt as to the deep interest which attaches to the theme we have chosen, nor has any "Pleasantrie" yet appeared, whose failure can be commensurate with that which may recoil on the rash individual, who now ventures on "popping the question," in the hope of its meeting the answer of success.

In looking around among the thousands of staid old couples, who must, at some time or other, have been privy to the *pop*, we are naturally led to speculate on the particular *mode* in which the matter may have been effected in each case respectively. Let us, even now, take a moment's survey of the assembly before us.

Is it possible that yon downcast example of abashed Jerry-ism, from whom, one would suppose, nothing could ever emanate except the passive phantom of self-mistrust —is it possible that he, borne onward by his own free-will, can have been so goaded by the spur of fashion, as to plunge into the fearful extremity of DECLARING HIMSELF? —of declaring himself to yon buxom specimen of absolute she-rule? Did *he* " pop the question?" If so, then follows the question, How did he pop it? Perhaps he popped it into the twopenny post-box, and felt suddenly as if he had put his leg into a man-trap; and went to the post-office half an hour after, in repentant terror, to

---
* From Blue Friar Pleasantries, *Fraser*, August, 1840.

try and get it out again, saying he had *mis*-directed it—which was true enough, though not to be helped, for it was already stamped the property of the *miss* to whom it was directed, and to whom, in half an hour more, it was delivered!

And, oh!—that double knock! "How is it with him, when every noise appals him!" Is it hope, or fear? and does the hope or the fear attach to the "yes" or the "no?" It *is* the postman! He tries to take up two-pence from the mantel-shelf; but the coppers dance under his agitated fingering, and half the money rolls under the fender; and he and the postman get alike impatient, while the girl keeps on, never finding the stray halfpence. He is, at length, alone. He breaks the seal! A positive statement of acceptance or denial might have been fatal to his wits; but it fortunately happens, on the contrary, that his wits have more than enough to do in discovering what the note actually means; and it is only on the opportune arrival of his confidential friend, that he is made to read it, as decidedly meaning "rather more yes than no." It is not our province to follow this case any further.

And—there's another. Behold yon angular-featured, bony-framed piece of living machinery, with all the sombre expression and deliberate power of a steam engine; abstracted in look; his thought ever working, like the huge rod of a mine-shaft, in communion with the unfathomable depths of material philosophy! What could induce *his* alliance with that delicate and gentle-looking creature, who thrives beside him like jessamine against the gable end of an iron-foundry? Studious at school, distinguished at college, and (as far as the world has seen him) ever engaged in exhibiting the practical results of his knowledge and sleepless speculation, when can *he* have found time to "tread the primrose path of dalliance?" When can "natural philosophy" have left *him* open to the insidious persuasions of natural affection? During what brief and accidental interval of relaxation did the quicksilver of love amalgamate with the gold of wisdom? Assuredly, he must have been lecturing upon the laws of gravity, when the little god of lightness shot him through the eyes of one who was not only his most attentive listener, but also, in his immediate estimation, the fairest. And then, doubtless, did our philosopher learn how to estimate Biron's* distinction between those "slow 'arts" which "entirely keep the brain" and that which

> "—— learned in a lady's eyes,
> Lives not alone immured in the head;
> But, with the motion of all elements,
> Courses as swift as thought in every power;
> And gives to every power a double power
> Above their functions and their offices!"

Well; in love let us grant him, then. How did *he* pop the question? He never made morning calls. He never attended evening parties. He never shunned *high*-ways in search of *by*-ways. He never went to pic-nics to discuss sandwiches and sentiment under wide-spreading beech-trees. He never joined water-parties, save once; nor was he ever left alone with his lady, save once: but these "onces" were simultaneous, and then must have occurred the mischief! Now, you will, of course, speculate on their having been left in a boat, while the boatman or their companions went for a while ashore—a situation, we grant, involving the extreme probability of the question being popped. Not so. It is morally impossible that *such* a man can have yielded himself up to so lazy a proceeding. Whatever the issue, there *must* have been some philosophy in the motive. We have already con-

---

* Shakspeare's "Biron."

cluded on his having been charmed with her attention and aptitude as his pupil. We have ventured, too, on the expression of our conviction, that he himself became subject to the pupil—of her eye—that *pupil* which masters professorship, and makes it in turn profess itself, not pupil only, but veriest slave. Still, the philosopher was only *so far* gone; and slaves have, ere now, thrown off their chains. Only once at a water-party; and only once alone with his lady? and both "onces" simultaneous; and *then* must have occurred the mischief! To explain —albeit "in supposition": the idea being romantic, the ballad style of information is indispensable:—

THE DIVING-BELLE.

"It looks fair above," to the lady he said;
"Let us haste in a boat to the Breakwater's head;
Thence we'll plunge in the deep. 'Twill delight you and me
To see *how* it looks in the depths of the sea."

They descended together; they fathomed the deep:
Securely shut in from the world's prying peep;
Said the gentleman,"Ne'er was't imagined by me,
Such a treasure to find in the depths of the sea!"

The lady she blush'd, and the gentleman too.
Said the latter, "Time presses,—my words must be few.
Do you know what is coming?" She knew it full well:
So the QUESTION WAS POPPED in the diving-bell.

Next turn we to that rakish-looking young fellow, who appears to belong to every other body rather than the other half of his own. The "bone of his bone" and the "flesh of his flesh" seems to participate in little more than his skin and spare-rib. She sits as if reflecting on a *dream* that has recently passed. Her imagination still sees the envy of youth and the ambition of maidenhood selecting *her* for the lady of his love; while, in the modesty of self-depreciation, she can only wonder at his choice. In the difficulty of her belief lives her only reluctance to respond to his attentions, which are, however, urged on with such a determined eloquence, that before any "question" is put, the conclusion is unquestionable. She remembers no particular time or formal circumstance of declaration. She only recollects a brief period, too violent for happiness. We need not pursue the "question" any further. It has not answered.

Far more encouraging is the aspect of the old couple now before us,—living realisations of a picture of social happiness,—a perfect lady and a perfect gentleman, carrying the romance of courtship into the later stage of matrimony,—" a pattern to these younger times,"—with personal beauty living to the last, because ever sustained by the staminal support of good temper, good sense, cheerful virtue, and easy circumstances,—which latter, by the way, have very much to do with it. Look at him, with his powdered head, and face of manly cut and colour ; true to his blue coat, buff waistcoat, and sound principles—religious and political. Behold him, not merely attending, as bound by law and custom, but gal-*lant*-ly escorting his lady-love *to* church, and never forgetting the day when he first escorted her *from* it. Ah, happy, depend upon it, were the circumstances under which *he* " popped the question." Like the last subject of our speculation, he was assured before he ventured ; but he was assured on more points than the *lady's* affection,—he was assured of his *own*. On both sides, a well-founded admiration, ripening into esteem ; and then, not bursting into madness, but mellowing into love. A corresponding scale of rank and education, sufficient affluence, sufficient beauty, and, at the time, no more than matured youth. It is likely they knew each other from their infancy, and had flirted with one another, before they were aware what "flirting" meant. It is likely the lady, when she was not more than five years old, had *patronised* the gentleman when he was not less than ten; and had, with all the "awful" simplicity of innocent childhood, declared to his father, that she "wished to have Dick for her husband." Dick, most likely, looked rather abashed by the declaration at the time; but time wears out the daring of little-girlhood, and the dulness of little-boyhood; and the day arrived when Dora, in her turn, was to look "abashed" at Dick's reminding her of that declaration, and stating his willingness to submit to it. And then did the "sisterly regard," which had existed through the major part of her "teens," begin to "veil itself" in the gracefully-hanging gauze of a delicate propriety. The "regard," however, continued to exist, never-the-*less*,—something the *more*; and when the now emboldened Dick repeated the readiness of his submission, it sounded so like the earnestness of a beseeching, that our once little lady-patroness could only answer with a slight trepidation, and a gentle blush. All this had been brought about too gradually to be evanescent; and it was too rational, too suitable in every respect as it regarded the lovers, and too advantageous in mere matters of family property and alliance, to be discountenanced by the fathers and mothers. So the preliminaries, sentimental, parental, and legal, being duly settled, the marriage may be supposed to be approaching, and all things just as regular as though there had been no romance in the case. Depend upon it, however, there is a possible union between passion and philosophy—between *ecsta*-tics and *mathema*-tics; and that, although Sir Richard may have married with a due regard to the absolute necessity of good family and fortune, he may still have been capable of "popping" the question, as follows:—

"Good morrow, my dear Dora" (said
The youth, in tones more soft than ever).

"Have you forgotten, gentle maid?
  Those words will 'scape *my* memory never.

I knew a little girl of five,
  Who told a little boy of ten,
She'd be his mate when he should wive;
  He wishes now—what *she* wished then.

O let not years destroy the love
  That infancy declared so sweetly:
If ever match was made above,
  If ever match was made discreetly—

'Twas on that bright approving day
  When first we met 'among the heather,'
Exchanging wild flowers on our way,
  As hand in hand we sped together.

Then say again, my Dora dear,
  What 'little Dick' deem'd passing sweet, love!
What, once abashed, *he* blushed to hear,
  O why dost *thou* blush to repeat, love?"

And so much for Sir Richard's way of "popping the question."

We are next engaged by a couple not less well suited than the former,—nay, even more closely allied in mutual resemblance. It has been occasionally asserted, that people will fall in love with some general likeness of themselves discoverable in the object of their admiration. The lady and gentleman before us resemble each other, just as we conceive might be the case with two pictures painted by one hand, and that the hand of a mannerist. They are now of a certain age; but they must have been remarkably handsome. Surely, it must be this couple of whom report speaks, when relating the story of a young lady and gentleman of the old school, who met, under peculiar circumstances, in the studio of a celebrated portrait-painter.

The artist was, at the same period, engaged upon the portraits of both, and painted them as a pair, without any further design than that of making them companion pictures for the exhibition of the Royal Academy, where, by permission of both sitters, he was to be allowed to hang them. Such was the accidental coincidence of the subjects as to the required style of picture, its composition, size, and tone of colour, that he resolved on finishing them from the same palette; and, further, "that the comparison might stand more proper," he placed them in temporary alliance, side by side, within the same frame,—a large, old, horizontal landscape frame, which exactly held them, and no room to spare between. Innocent of any intent beyond that of artistical harmony, he was busily employed in giving his finishing touches to the one and the other alternately, and had just brought them into a condition of the most perfect and mutual sympathy, when a ring at his bell announced the arrival of one of his sitters; it was little matter which, for he was ready for either.

There was a pause. He heard the hall door open; but, instead of the usual ready step of the lady *or* the gentleman, making her or his way up the stairs, he heard the lady *and* the gentleman bandying courtesies in the porch. The gentleman had rung first, and the lady had arrived just as the door was opened. The gentleman immediately advanced to hand her from her carriage, and to yield precedence to her as the painters' visitor. The lady could not think of such a thing. The gentleman could not think of anything else. "But your business is urgent?" said the lady, "and I can most conveniently occupy myself for half an hour in calling upon some friends a little further on." "Nay," replied the gentleman, "then you will compel me to leave the house. I am merely calling, *en passant*, to look at a portrait, which, I believe, requires nothing more from me than a final approval;" to which the lady answered, it was precisely her own case; and so, at length, they resolved on making their call simultaneously.

As the reader may anticipate, although they had never met before, they had recognised each other at the first moment of their meeting; for they were scarcely more like themselves than their likenesses; and each had been in the habit of contemplating the other's portrait, as the chief object of interest while sitting for their own. Often had the gentleman expatiated on what must be the charms of the portrait's *lady*, as a work of *heart*; while the lady had more than once delicately hinted at the beauty of the gentleman's *portrait*, as a work of *art*. The painter had, moreover, let each into the secret of the other's family; and he had a great deal to say about the possessions, pretensions, and high character of both. It must be confessed, their mutual recognition, taken in connexion with the prospect awaiting them in the painter's studio, forms a neat little bit of practical romance; and nothing now remains, but at once to bring our story to the climax of their jointly entering the artist's room, and discovering, in an instant, how indisputably they were " framed " for one another. We might dilate upon the gentleman's emotion, the lady's confusion, and the painter's innocent amazement; but we should only swell the interval to the impatience of our reader, who must necessarily insist upon the conclusion, that the gentleman would say, in due time:—

> A pity 't were, my gentle fair,
> These portraits should divide;
> Then be 't thy will, that they may still,
> Hang fondly side by side!
>
> So sweetly see, their smiles agree,
> As they had plighted troth;
> His love so true, enough for two—
> Her loveliness for both.

> Let that and this unite in bliss,
> Or augury be blam'd ;
> We are, 't is clear, as pictur'd here,
> For mutual comfort fram'd.

It were next curious to consider, how that exceedingly unlovely and very self-satisfied elderly gentleman, could have rendered himself the chosen suitor of his pretty young wife, while it is well known that the good-looking young man in the corner was her professed admirer at the same time. It is also rumoured on good authority, that "the question was popped" by both; that the youthful wooer went simply in his best coat, while the other went in his new carriage. The first was, most likely, too agitated to speak, so he addressed the lady on gilt satin note-paper as follows :—

> Madam,—Under the depressing sense of my own unworthiness and presumption, I fear my speech might falter, and leave my unqualified admiration imperfectly uttered.
> I therefore resolve on silently presenting to you on my knee this written homage of my heart, in the hope that you will bid me rise from my devotion the happiest man upon earth.
>
> Yours, &c.

"Pray rise, sir," says the inexorable fair one, "and brush the dust from your too-humbled knee. I have only to regret you should have been ignorant of my already confirmed engagement to another."

Which "engagement" was entered into at least twenty minutes before, when the elderly gentleman emerged from his chariot—all collar, cravat, shirtfrill, and gaiters; at once "popped the question," backed his suit with a note of recommendation signed on behalf of the Governors and Company of the Bank of England; obtained the acceptance of the "pa" and the "ma;" and then hobbled away as fast as his premature infirmities would allow, crying, "Hey for the wedding!"

One of the most amusing records connected with our

present subject, is to be found in the chronicles of the Civil Wars in the time of Charles. A knightly royalist bachelor, separated from his companions, was sore pressed by the determined vengeance of some half-dozen Cromwellists. Not being (like the veteran Dentatus of old) a hero of muscular might, he was content "to be a man of valour, without showing it;" and, at all events, made such good use of his heels, that he outran his ferocious pursuers by the length of a musket-shot. Being, however, a little man of some years and much fat, heavily encumbered, too, with his helmet, sword, and buckler, his breathing had now become as short as his legs, and he felt that his only chance was to rush through the ready-opened door of a house before him, with a view to concealment. The servants of the house were " up and doing;" but not so the two maiden mistresses, who were still side by side in one bed; and, having been awake all night, under the apprehension of what royalty and virginity might suffer, had just fallen asleep, to dwell on the fate of the Sabine women, and to speculate on what might be their own. Judge, then, of their horror, when they were suddenly aroused by the appearance of an armed man, wearing a sheath with a sword in it! But he was *not* a Cromwellite. No; *there* were the face and figure of the loyal Sir Richard Spriggins, who had scarcely breath to utter, "Ladies! for the sake of Heaven and the king, protect me from the assassins who are close at my heels! Hark! they are at the door!—they are ascending the stairs! They will respect the sanctity of your bed, so long, at least, as you remain in it; so, let me jump in for a few moments' concealment, and, by my loyalty, I'll marry either of you, as you shall settle it between you!" "Well, settle *yourself* between us, *now*," said the maidens; and, in another minute, there were three or four savage-looking assassins peering into every cupboard and corner, poking their long swords up the chimney, behind, above, and under the bed; and, in short, everywhere except *within* the bed, where warmly, snugly, lay the knight, affording a matchless example of the *shifts* by which men sometimes avoid ruin, and by which women as often procure husbands.

It is a great thing to be sure of the weather when you start on a "popping" excursion. Our good friend, B——, was too unmindful of this when he sallied forth, one very windy day, to escort the lady of his choice from her father's house at the bottom of the hill, to her uncle's at the top. He was one of your very particular men, who especially abhor those undignifying accidents which are so constantly reminding us that there is but one step from the romantic to the ridiculous. In every circumstance connected with woman, he was particularly anxious that there should be a perfection of elegance and princely grace. Having allowed himself, rather carelessly, to fall in love, it was now his earnest resolve to make up for his folly, by the exquisite care with which that love should be declared. His conversation began to assume an elegantly courteous tone, as he accompanied the lady along the foot of the hill; and as they, step by step, ascended, his language became correspondingly elevated from courtesy to compliment—from compliment to solicitude—from solicitude to tenderness—from tenderness to earnestness—from earnestness to passion--and from passion towards declaration—when, at the moment the "pop" was on his tongue, off went his hat in a gust of wind! and away went the lover all down the hill after it, leaving the lady, however, assured of his intentions, and convulsed with laughter at his mischance.

Truly, if kind Fortune did not often provide opportunities, many are the modest men who would remain unprovided with wives. Numerous had been the speeches declaratory, composed and rehearsed by our poor cousin Paul; and many times (and in as many forms) had the "question" been *put* upon paper; but never yet, in any form whatever, had it been "popped" to the lady. The latter was one of those gentle *philanthropists* who feel charitably towards *man*-kind; and it was, therefore, reasonable to expect, that (supposing nothing really objectionable in person, mind, or morals) she would yield a not very hesitating "Yes" to the first young man who should ask for it. It has been asserted, that she more than once said to herself, " If Peter *should* ask me, I do not think I should say ' No'; and if Paul should *entreat* me, I really think I should say ' Yes.' "

As to Peter, he only hesitated from a cautious regard to his *own* value, as who should say, " I must not throw myself away. I must see that this pretty damsel is worthy of me." Poor Paul, on the contrary, rated himself at the lowest; and would still have continued " letting *I dare not* wait upon *I would*," had it not been for one of the most " blessed haps " that ever favoured swain forlorn !

To relieve his love-racked thoughts, he had one day mingled in the crowd of the Polytechnic Hall, in Regent Street, where Philosophy puts on his gayest attire, and becomes the amusing host of beauty, fashion, and playful childhood. Paul was standing among the crowd, near one of the " metallic reflectors," having just read the account of their efficiency in the transmission of whispers through a distance of one hundred feet (*vide* bill), when he saw the woman of his heart and the man of his hate talking together before the reflector at the other end of the gallery. As he contemplated this most disagreeable indication, he saw the odious Peter suddenly resign the arm of the fair one, and advance towards the

P

reflector by which he was himself standing, leaving the lady to adjust her position near the other, so as to hear the intended whisper. Judge, then, of her surprise, when, instead of the expected *Peter's* communication, she heard the following : " Mary—Mary—it is *Paul* who speaks: in one word, to avow the love which he has long felt, though he has never had the courage to declare it till now! Oh, answer me! answer but a syllable! Here comes my detested rival !"

It must not be expected that Mary could answer "Yea" with quite such lightning speed; but she looked round—recognised Paul (who looked as if he had, at least, committed murder)—made up her mind, at all events, *not* to have Peter—and had presence of mind to regain her position as a listener, just as her late companion had taken his as her opposite. Poor Paul, choked by the utterance of his swollen heart, had, in the meanwhile, mingled in the crowd to conceal his confusion. "Do you hear me?" whispered Peter. " Perfectly well," said the maiden. " Shall I return?" asked the gentleman. " Don't hurry yourself," replied the lady. Peter looked round; the lady was gone. She shortly rejoined him; but not till she had given the bewildered Paul a *glance* as perfectly affirmative as if she had *whispered* " Yes."

There is a pretty story of two ladies, who were observed by a gentleman, standing near one of the entrances of Kensington Gardens, exposed to a sharp shower, and vainly looking for their carriage, which they had expected to find ready in waiting. The gentleman's carriage, however, was at hand, as his politeness ever was. His card was immediately tendered with the offer of his splendid equipage, which was too earnestly made, and too imperatively enforced by the rude compulsion of the boisterous weather, to be refused. When the ladies were seated, he requested their directions for his coachman, stating that he would wait at the house of a friend close by until the return of his carriage; and then followed a not-to-be-resisted invitation that he would take a seat in his own vehicle; "For," said the elder of the lovely twain, "*our* way, my lord, is yours. Permit me to announce myself as Mrs. ***, and this lady as my sister, Miss ——." They proceeded homeward. "It is the most easy carriage I ever travelled in," said Miss ——. "Indeed, madam," said my lord, "it is, nevertheless, but a jolting conveyance to one like myself, doomed to the rough by-road of bachelorship." This produced a little beautiful confusion at the time. The "pop" was "too unadvised—too sudden;" and the "question" required at least six weeks to work itself into positive form; but the result was a matter of certainty from the first, and the "easiest of carriages," at the end of six weeks more, was seen at the door of St. George's, Hanover Square, awaiting the loveliest of brides and her lord—a *bachelor* no longer.

We have also known examples of gallant gentlemen "popping" umbrellas over bonnets in distress, and anon "popping questions" under umbrellas. We might likewise instance the *pop*-acious influence of covered archways and pastry-cooks' shops—havens in stress of weather, not only for boys and girls, but sometimes for Cupid himself; who, if the storm outlives his patience, will shoot an arrow by way of pastime. Even churches exclude him not; and when two hands belonging to different sexes are engaged in holding one prayer-book, it is surprising how the pages *persist* in opening at, "Wilt thou have this man," etc. Weddings have a considerable influence in the promoting of "pops." Your bridesmaids are especially liable to be *made brides*. Whether truly or not, they always *seem*, from their dress, agitation, and the very complexion of their gentle office, predisposed to the reception of *pop*-o-sitions. The actual ceremony of marriage is, perhaps, less stimulating than the breakfast which follows, where there is so much sugared cake, and so many "merry thoughts" to be broken. Our friend, Jack Hastings, was the victim of a wedding-breakfast. He attended the marriage of his friend, and straightway fell in love with the sister of his friend's bride. They pulled against each other with the breast-bone of a chicken. The gentleman retained the larger half: so far, *he* was to be married first. They next drew lots for precedence, and lo! the *lady* gained the day. " It is a drawn game," said the gentleman—"so let us be married *together*." "At the same *time*, you mean," said the bridesmaid. "With the same *ring*, if you please," said the youth; and so *he* " popped the question." Whether she accepted him or not is *out* of the "question"; but you shall know. We have said he was the "victim" of a wedding-breakfast. May we then say that he "achieved" the maid he sought? Not so. The conclusion is a sad one. She was reluctant to reply to him. He pressed his suit the more earnestly. " I will to-morrow," said he, " ask you a simple question touching some ordinary topic of the day. If you say 'Yes' to *that*, I shall construe it as applying to the question I have just put to you. If 'No,' I must bear it as best I may." The morning came—to *him* after a sleepless night. He descended into the breakfast-room, where sat the object of his admiration among her relatives and friends. She was absorbed in the thoughtless converse of the moment, and scarcely noticed who it was that asked her " If she intended to ride in the park as usual?" "Yes," she replied; and the questioner remained in an ecstasy of joy for at least half an hour; when his manner reminded her of what she had, unfortunately, been too forgetful.

She was compelled to undeceive him, by giving him to understand that she *should* have answered "No." Alas! poor Jack! He never loved again! Yet do not too deeply distress yourself in his fate; for he has contrived to become a very old bachelor; while the lady, too, has lived to become a very decided old maid. They meet occasionally, and sometimes venture to participate in a "merry thought" of their youthful follies; but it is always a very formal attempt; and each of them looks as if there were a *bone* in the throat.

We forget where we met with the following laconic example of " popping the question :"—

" Pray, madam, do you like buttered toast ?"

" Yes, sir."

" Buttered on both sides ?"

" Yes, sir."

" Will you marry me ?"

The mode adopted by a certain eccentric physician is almost as condensed. A lady came to consult him. He prescribed and took his guinea. " Madam," said he, " I wish to see you again this time to-morrow. In the interval, take the medicine here prescribed, and, ere we meet again, make up your mind to give a plain 'yes' or 'no' to the question I now put to you. I am inclined to wed, but have no time to woo. Will you allow me to lay out my fee in the purchase of your wedding-ring ?"

Contrastingly with the foregoing, we give the following:—A young man of great personal beauty, accomplishment, and fortune, had been staying a few days in the house of a friend, whose sister's charms were not less conspicuous than those of the knightly visitor. Some persons fancy themselves in love before they are so; but, in the present instance, no such false persuasion seems to have existed, for, when the youth took his departure, he bade " farewell " to his host and late companions, with no other feeling than that of leaving a place where he had been—happy, certainly—*superlatively* happy; but, up to that moment, unconscious of any exclusively particular cause for being so. The company and the entertainments had been *all* charming in their respective ways, and the cheerfulness so incessant and unfailing, as to preclude any opportunity for mere sentimental indulgence. Even the leave-taking went off in a flash of joyous excitement. The departing guest shook hands with all; and, amidst the cracking of the postilion's whips, and a dozen simultaneous " God be with you's," his carriage moved off in a gallop.

" Hey day!" said the youth, experiencing a sudden qualm of feeling—

" My heart is heavy, as, just now, 'twas light!"

When he arrived at the lodge-gate, he contrived to remember that he had forgotten a small packet which he had promised to bear from the pretty sister to her cousin; so, " Egad, boys!" said he, " you must drive back."

As the carriage was returning up the avenue, he saw —unseen—the whole party (as he thought) entering the woods, at a quarter of a mile distance on the other side of the house. A moment more, and they vanished. Why should he feel so disappointed, and sigh so heavily? "I must, however, get the packet," said he, "at all events." So the carriage drove up to the door.

He looked up, and saw—

Oh, what was his emotion at that moment!

The sash of a window was thrown up, and the softest of voices, emanating from the sweetest of lips, exclaimed, "What!—Mr. Ernest—returned!"

Her eye was moist, as with weeping; and before she spoke, he had observed her hastily apply her handkerchief, and as quickly conceal it again.

"I have," said he, "most unpardonably forgotten the packet you engaged me to deliver, and am come back to procure it."

"Oh!" she replied, "I am grieved you should have so troubled yourself; for it was of such little import, that I had forgotten to get it ready."

"Then pray let me wait," said he, "till you have prepared it."

And then he learned that all, save herself, were "gone for a walk" in the woods; so he left his carriage, promising to wait in the library till the packet should be ready; and he *did* wait—for two minutes, at least—which, by the way, seemed to him considerably more than ten; and at length the young lady appeared, with a blush and trembling hand, to deliver the packet, which he, with a blush and trembling hand, received.

Well, he had obtained what he returned for; why not again depart? But, no; he could not, for his life! so, for a moment's excuse, he asked how it happened *she* was not of the walking-party? and, there being more emotion than reason in the faltering words of her reply, he bethought him of saying, how truly he was to be congratulated on the neglect, which had caused his return for "at least, one more interview with *her*." She could but say "he flattered her too much"; and he could but reply by saying, as he gently and almost unconsciously took her hand, "would that she could flatter *him* by acknowledging, that his return was not unwelcome."

Oh, what precious moments were those! The house, ere now, ringing with the mirth of a numerous and thoughtless company; and now, still in the absence of all, save the silent eloquence of two self-convicted lovers! There is something, too, in a library, peculiarly suited to such an occasion. In the first place, it is always the warmest and most genial-looking room in a large mansion, and predisposes the heart to feelings of gentleness. In the next place, its distinguishing furniture—its books, with their gilded backs beaming and glittering in the firelight; filled (so many of them) with tales of romance and passion, and Love the ruling theme. All this inclines the mind, if there be poetry in it, to take an imaginative turn, and especially to repose on such an opportunity as that we are now describing.

* * * * * *

Again the carriage rattles down the avenue with a lone, but happy lover in it; and, in gentle meditation by the library fireside, her hand still holding the locket he has left her, and her lip sensible of his parting kiss, sits she who has made that lover happy.

But the packet is forgotten, after all.

THE BLUE BOX.

APPENDIX.

Some particulars respecting two other members of the Order have come to hand while the final pages of this book were being prepared, and these, in accordance with our promise on page 86, we embody in this brief appendix.

From Mr. John Best Newton (who writes from Luleå°, Sweden), we have received the following interesting biographical notes respecting his father, Mr. Thomas Duncan Newton (Brother Roger). It may be remembered that Mr. J. B. Newton was himself elected a Lay Brother of the Order, by the monastic title of Brother Optimus (see page 44). He is therefore the only survivor of the Blue Friars, and was, we believe, at one time the possessor of many relics of the Venerable Order. He says:—

"My father was born at Weymouth in 1799. The family came to Plymouth in connection with the appointment of his father (John Newton) to the chief place in the Custom House service there. I do not know the date. His mother was a Miss Cole, of a Cornish family. The family lived in George Street, Plymouth, when that was the fashionable west end of the town: the first private carriage owned in Plymouth was kept by his mother. My father in 1835 married the eldest daughter of Thomas Gill, of Tavistock, afterwards well known as M.P. for Plymouth, and originator of many commercial enterprises in the vicinity.

"Their first establishment was at 11 Lockyer Street, afterwards, in 1860, removing to West Hoe Terrace.

"The Lockyer Street residence was the one associated with Blue Friar memories. My father was educated at Totnes Grammar School, and afterwards studied for the law, was enrolled as a solicitor, but never practised. He was a man of decidedly artistic temperament, with considerable knowledge of, and taste for, music; he was one of the principal members of the Plymouth "Glee and Madrigal Club," who met in turn at the members' houses for a studiously simple dinner and an evening's music. His sense of humour was great, and his powers of mimicry above the common order; he was, moreover, a past master of anecdotal conversation, which brought into play both talents, and made his society sought for at all social gatherings.

"His special "chum" in B. F. society was George Wightwick, whom he greatly esteemed. This gentleman lived in Athenæum Terrace, and went so far as to have a private B. F. bell at his front door, undiscoverable by the uninitiated. William Snow Harris he always described as being spoilt as a Blue Friar by his scientific pursuits, and his anxiety to wring honour and reward from a reluctant Government, for his services to them.

" My father was in person what they used to call ' a pretty man,'— a man somewhat easily led, always good-natured and easy-going, qualities which were taken advantage of by those professing to be his friends.

" His relations on his father's side were exceedingly few in number, and consisted principally of the Brideslowe family, resident at Millaton House. Those on his mother's side were more numerous, but with the exception of his uncle, Thomas Cole (who resided almost exactly opposite to the George Street house), he had not much intercourse with them. His death occurred in 1869, he having lost my mother five years previously.

" I have a distinct recollection of my appearance at the B. F. meeting when I was brought in in my mother's arms. There was a tree in a large tub in the room, with the owl and magpie perched up in it: the bottles on the table were covered by a kind of ' cosey ' or cover, consisting of either a priest or nun in long dresses which hid it from view. There were more than the sacred " W.H.I.N." in the room, but *who* they were I could not say. That the meetings were not a mere feast is evidenced by the rules enjoining the simplicity of the entertainment. I believe Jacobson to have been really the ablest man, but I have no recollection of him.

" My father kept up his acquaintance with Charles Mathews to the last. I was with him when he called on him in Cheltenham, shortly before his (C. M.'s) death. He sent in a card about two feet square with his B. F. name on it !"

Mr. Edwin Lovell-Lovell writes :—

" The only definite information I can give concerning my father is that he was born 7th May, 1808, and died 21st May, 1877. He was educated at Eton, and appointed Clerk of the Peace for the county of Somerset on the 13th of August, 1846, by the Right Honourable Lord Portman, Lord Lieutenant for the county. He held other minor appointments."

Mr. Lovell resided at Sharcombe House, Dinder, near Wells, and it was at a sale of books and other effects at that place in February, 1887, that the " Book of the Records " which forms the substance of the first portion of this volume, was purchased. All the other papers, together with much of the paraphernalia of the Order, came into the possession of the son of Brother Glastonbury, who now resides at Barnes, near London.

LIST OF SUBSCRIBERS.

Aldridge, Dr., Plympton
Alger, W. H., Stoke
Allen, J., Plymouth
Andrews, W., F.R.H.S., Hull
Anthony, Rev. F. E., M.A., Plymouth
Athenæum Club, London (per H. R. Tedder)
Attwood, J. S., Plymouth (2 copies)
Axon, William E. A., Manchester

Back, J., Plymouth
Bailey, Alderman W. H., Salford (6 copies)
Bailey, H. J., Stonehouse
Balmain, Rollo, Plymouth
Ballinger, John, Cardiff
Baring-Gould, Rev. S., M.A., Lew Trenchard
Barrett, F. T., Glasgow
Bartlett, E., Plymouth
Bate, C. Spence, F.R.S., Plymouth
Bayly, John, Plymouth (5 copies)
Bayly, R., J.P., Plymouth
Bazley, R. J., Plymouth
Bennett, J. N., Plymouth (2 copies)
Bewes, Rev. Thomas A., Plymouth (2 copies)
Binns, Rev. W., Plymouth
Birch, C. B., A.R.A., London
Birmingham Free Library (per J. D. Mullins)
Birmingham, W., Plymouth (6 copies)
Blackledge, W., London (2 copies)
Boase, G. C., London
Boger, Rev. Canon E., London
Bond, J. T., Plymouth
Bowring, L. B., Torquay
Bright, R. E., Plymouth
Briscoe, J. Potter, Nottingham (2 copies)
Bristol Free Library (per John Taylor)
Broadley, A. M., London
Broadmead, W. B., Bridgwater
Brown, J. P., Plymouth
Brushfield, Dr. T. N., Budleigh-Salterton
Bulteel, Thomas, Radford
Burnard, C. F., J.P., Plymouth (2 copies)
Burnard, R., Plymouth
Bush, Rev. Canon Paul, Duloe Rectory, Cornwall

Clifford, Right Hon. Lord, Ugbrooke, Chudleigh
Cann, Mark, Plymouth
Cann, William, Philipsburg, U.S.A.
Cawthorn & Hutt, Messrs., London
Chanter, J. R., Barnstaple

Chapple, Edwin, Plymouth (2 copies)
Chatterton, Dr., Plymouth
Chivers, Cedric, Bath
Clark, Henry, Efford Manor
Clark, J. B., Tavistock (2 copies)
Clinch, G., British Museum, London
Cole, Ralph, London
Cole, Miss Emily, Teignmouth
Collier, Arthur B., Callington
Collier, J. F., Liverpool
Collier, Mortimer J., Horrabridge
Collier, W. F., J.P., Horrabridge
Collins-Splatt, H., Brixton
Commin, J. G., Exeter (12 copies)
Coulthard, Mrs., Plymstock
Courtney, W. P., London
Cranford, R., Dartmouth (2 copies)
Crisp, F. A., London
Croft, C. W., Plymouth
Crossing, W., South Brent

Davis, Orlando J. H., Plymouth
Day, Charles, London
Derry, William, Plymouth
Digby, W., C.I.E., Beckenham, Kent
Dobson, Austin, London
Douthwaite, W. R., London
Doveton, F. B., London
Downing, William, Birmingham (3 copies)
Drake, Dr. H. H., London
Drake, W. H., Jersey
Dredge, Rev. J. Ingle, Buckland Brewer
Dustow, Mrs. S. K., Stonehouse

Ebrington, Viscount, M.P., J.P., Southmolton
Eliot, Col. the Hon. C., London
Eden, G., Plymouth
Edye, Major L., Walmer
Embry, J. H., Stoke

Faull, A. C., Plymouth
Fincham, H. W., London
Firks, G., Plymouth
Folkard, H. T., Wigan
Fortescue, J. F., J.P., Plymouth
Foster, E., Newton Abbot
Foster, J. B., Plymouth
Fribourg & Freyer, Messrs., London (2 copies)
Frost, W. A., London

Garland, G., Bodmin
Gidley, G., Plymouth
Gilbert, H. M., Southampton
Glasse, Mrs., Plymstock

Grafton, Miss R., London
Gray, Henry, London (2 copies)
Greenwood, Thomas, F.R.G.S., London
Gribble, H. A., M.R.I.B.A., London

Hamilton, A. H. A., F.S.A., Exeter
Harper, T., Plymouth
Harris, Augustus, London
Harris, Miss Snow, Plymouth
Harrison, W., Plymouth
Hartnoll, A. E., Newquay
Harvey, Rev. Julian, Plymouth
Hawken, G., Plymouth
Haydon, G. H., London (2 copies)
Hayne, Rev. Prebendary, M.A., Buckland Monachorum
Healey, W. B., London
Hems, Harry, Exeter
Hingston, Alfred, J.P., Plymouth
Holborn, R. M., London
Hughan, W. J., Torquay
Hughes, Thomas, F.S.A., Chester
Hume, John, Santiago, Chili
Humphery, G. R., London
Hurrell, J. S., Kingsbridge

Iago, Rev. W., B.A., Bodmin
Inskip, Capt. G. H., R.N., J.P., Plymouth
Iredale, A., Torquay (6 copies)

Jago, Charles S., Plymouth
Jago, George, Plymouth
Jago, Miss, Plymouth
Jarrold & Sons, Messrs., Norwich
Jeffery, F. B., Plymouth
Jewers, T. D. A., Portsmouth
Jones, Miss, Saltash
Joynt, W. Lane, D.L., Dublin

Keats, J. H., Plymouth (2 copies)
Keys, I. W. N., Plymouth

Lopes, Right Hon. Sir Massey, Maristow
Lancaster, E. S, Plymouth
Lane, F. Cecil, Plymouth
Lane, John, Torquay
London Corporation Library, Guildhall (per C. Welch)
London Library (per R. Harrison)
Lord, J. R., Plymouth
Lovell, Edwin Lovell, Barnes (2 copies)
Lovell, Mrs., sen., London
Lowcay, Capt., R.N., Plymouth
Luke, Charles, Plymouth
Luke, W. H., Plymouth

Lyons, A. E., Stonehouse
Mount Edgcumbe, Right Hon. the Earl of
Morley, Right Hon. Earl of, Saltram
Monkswell, Lord, London
Mabin, Frank, Plymouth
M'Bain, J. M., Arbroath
McBryde, H. A., Plymouth
M'Cormick, Rev. F. H. J., Whitehaven
Marlow, Arthur L., London
Martin, John, Plymouth
Mason, Thomas, London (2 copies)
Mathews, C. Elkin, London
Mathews, E. R. N., Bristol
Matthews, Henry, Plymouth
Matthews, J. W., Plymouth
May, J. H. S., M.R.C.S., Plymouth
May, W. C., London
Meeres, Dr. E. E., Plymouth
Miles & Co., Messrs. T., London (2 copies)
Mitchell, F., Chard
Mitchell, Miss Maude, London
Mitchell, Philip, Plymouth
Moon, James E., Plymouth
Moore, Mrs. W. F., Plymouth
Moreton, H., F.C.O., Plymouth
Morrison, Walter, M.P., London
Moysey, John, Stoke
Mugford, J. A., Plymouth
Mullard, C. H., Plymouth
Murray, Frank, Derby

Noble, T. C., London
Newton, John Best, Lulea°, Sweden (2 copies)
Newton, T. W., London
Norman, John, Plymouth
Norrington, Charles, J.P., Plymouth
Norwich Free Library (per Mr. G. Easter)

ODD VOLUMES, MEMBERS OF YE SETTE—

   Ross, H. J. Gordon, President, London (2 copies)
   Brown, James Roberts, F.R.O.S. ,,
   East, Alfred ,,
   Elgar, Frank (2 copies) ,,
   Haité, George Charles, F.L.S. ,,
   Hamilton, Walter, F.R.G.S., F.R.H.S. ,,
   Lane, John ,,
   Moore, Henry, A.R.A. ,,
   Renton, Edward ,,
   Tyler, G. R. ,,
   Venables, T. C. ,,

ODD VOLUMES—*continued.*
  Vezin, Hermann, London
  Walford. Edward, M.A., London
  Welsh, Charles ,,
  Wyman, C. W. H. ,,

Ogle, J. J., Bootle

Phear, Sir J. B., Bart., Marpool, Exmouth
Pollock, Sir Fredk., London
Pagen, J. F., Plymouth
Pardew, John, Plymouth
Parlby, Rev. J. Hall, J.P., Plymouth
Pearce, G. B., Hayle
Pearce. W. E., London
Pearn, E. A., Plymouth
Penny, Rev. Dr., Plymouth
Perry, George B., Boston, U.S.A.
Pethick, John, J.P., Plymouth
Philp, R., Plymouth
Picken, Miss, Plymouth
Pitts, Col. Thos., Plymouth
Plant, Major John, Salford
Plymouth Co-operative Society
Plymouth Free Public Library
Prance, Dr. C. R., Plymouth
Prance, H. Penrose, Plymouth
Prideaux, Lieut.-Col., India
Pridham, E., Plymouth
Pridham, Glinn, London
Pridham-Wippell, P. H., London

Radford, D., Mount Tavy, Tavistock (2 copies)
Radford, John H., Plymouth (2 copies)
Randall, J., Sheffield
Randle, W., Stonehouse
Rashleigh, Evelyn W., Kilmarth, Par
Reader, Arthur, London (2 copies)
Redway, G., London
Reeves, J. Sims, London
Rendle, James, Plymouth
Rogers, W. H. H., F.S.A., Colyton
Rowe, J. Brooking, F.S.A., Plympton
Rundle, Charles, Plymouth

St. Germans, Right Hon. the Earl of, Port Eliot
Seale, Sir Henry P., Dartmouth
St. Aubyn, J. Piers, Marazion
St. Aubyn, Rev. W., M.A., Stoke Damerel
Scott, Miss S. L., Christchurch
Scott, Rev. Prebendary, M.A., Stonehouse
Seale-Hayne, C., M.P., London
Seaton, S., Plymouth

Sellick, G. H., Plymouth (3 copies)
Shelly, John, Plymouth
Short, John, Plymouth
Smith, J. H., Plymouth
Smith, W. H. & Sons, London (4 copies)
Square, W. J., Plymouth
Stanlake, R., Plymouth
Stevens, Henry, London (2 copies)
Stilwell, J. P., London
Story, Edward, London
Stribley, E., Plymouth
Sutton, C. W., Manchester

Taylor, John, Bristol
Taylor, John, Plymouth
Thomson, E. B., M.D., Plymouth
Trevail, Silvanus, Truro
Trevor-Roper, Mrs. E. C., Okehampton
Tucker, Henry, Plymouth

Varnier, A. H., Plymouth
Vicary, William, Stonehouse

Wade, W. Cecil, Plymouth
Walker, W. H., Plymouth
Wall, A. B., Cheltenham
Wall, W. Price, Exeter
Waring, H. J., J.P., Mayor of Plymouth (2 copies)
Watts, R. I., J.P., Mayor of Devonport
Webb, F. J., Liverpool
Weeks, John, Plymouth
Were, Nicholas, Plymouth
Westcott, Leonard T., Valparaiso
White, T. J., London
White, W. P. H., Plymouth
Whiteford, C. C., Plymouth
Whiteford, Sidney T., London
Whitehead, J., London
Wightwick, Mrs., London (5 copies)
Wildridge, T. T., Hull
Wilkinson, Ven. Archdeacon, D.D., Plymouth
Willcocks, Dr. F., London
Williams, Major C. Woolmer, London
Williams, Rev. Philip, M.A., Plymouth
Wills, S. J., Helston
Wilson, J. F., London (2 copies)
Wilson, J. Walter, Plymouth
Windeatt, E., Totnes
Wonnacott, John, Liskeard
Wood, J. E., Plymouth
Woodhouse, H. B. S., Plymouth
Woollcombe, W. J., Plymouth

Zaehnsdorf, J. W., London

ADDITIONAL SUBSCRIBERS.

Acland, Sir Henry W., K.C.B., Oxford
Allen, Edward Hiron, Exeter
Amery, Fabyan, Ashburton

Bellamy, G. D., Plymouth (2 copies)
Blacker, Rev. Beaver H., M.A., Clifton

Cartwright, Rev. Anson, Teignmouth
Christie, Chancellor R. C., Roehampton, S.W.
Cross, T. H., Plymouth

Devon and Exeter Institution, Exeter (per E. Parfitt)

Emery, W., Plymouth

Fuge, Miss, Plymouth

Holme, Charles, London (*Member of Odd Volumes*)

Jarvis, J. W., London
Jeffreson, Mrs., Melbourne, Australia

Kearley, John, London
Kettle, D. W., F.R.G.S., London (*Member of Odd Volumes*)
Knill, William, North Devon Athenæum, Barnstaple

Liskeard Literary Institution (per C. W. Jewell)

Mare, G. F., Tavistock
Monk, J. E., Plymouth
Moore-Stevens, John C., J.P., Torrington

Pink, W. D., Leigh, Lancashire
Plymouth Institution
Plymouth Proprietary Library (per J. Whitmarsh)
Prynne, Mrs., Plymouth

Rawson, Harry, Manchester
Reed, Henry, Plymouth
Risk, Mrs., Plymouth

Sibbald, J. G. E., London
Snell, Henry J., Plymouth
Square, J. Elliot, Plymouth
Suffield, John, Birmingham

Trollope, T. Adolphus, Budleigh Salterton

Wade, Edwin R., Penryn
Welsford, W. C., London
Whipple, H. H., Plymouth
Wright, Mrs. Henry, Melbourne, Australia

Related Titles from Westphalia Press

Ancient Mysteries and Modern Masonry: The Collected Writings of Jewel P. Lightfoot, Edited by Billy J. Hamilton Jr.

Jewel P. Lightfoot. Former Attorney General of the State of Texas. Past Grand Master of the Masonic Grand Lodge of Texas. From humble beginnings in rural Arkansas, he worked to become an educated man who excelled in law and Freemasonry. He was a gentleman of his time, well-known as a scholar, public speaker, and Masonic philosopher.

Essay on The Mysteries and the True Object of The Brotherhood of Freemasons
by Jason Williams

This isn't a reprint of a classic. It's a new rendition with new life breathed into it, to be enjoyed both by the layperson trying to understand the Craft and Masonic scholars taking a deeper dive into the fraternity's golden years—when the concepts of liberty and equality were still fresh.

Female Emancipation and Masonic Membership:
An Essential Collection
By Guillermo De Los Reyes Heredia

Female Emancipation and Masonic Membership: An Essential Combination is a collection of essays on Freemasonry and gender that promotes a transatlantic discussion of the study of the history of women and Freemasonry and their contribution in different countries.

Freemasonry, Heir to the Enlightenment
by Cécile Révauger

Modern Freemasonry may have mythical roots in Solomon's time but is really the heir to the Enlightenment. Ever since the early eighteenth century freemasons have endeavored to convey the values of the Enlightenment in the cultural, political and religious fields, in Europe, the American colonies and the emerging United States.

Masonic Myths and Legends
by Pierre Mollier

Freemasonry preserves the teachings of a primitive Judeo-Christian gnosis. In order to better understand these legends and myths and their significance, Pierre Mollier has studied their origins and attempted to find their sources.

Exploring the Vault: Masonic Higher Degrees 1730–1800
by John Belton and Roger Dachez

The study adopted a forensic approach to the available evidence, and the discoveries exceeded expectations. The book details their 'archaeological finds' and offers a novel perspective on the development of the Higher Degrees during the eighteenth century.

Étienne Morin: From the French Rite to the Scottish Rite by Arturo de Hoyos and Josef Wäges

All extant Masonic records have been consulted and using this meta-data, a comprehensive reconstruction emerges, revealing that Étienne Morin was a founding masonic figure in Saint Domingue and creator of his own high degree system, that operated for a time as a defacto Grand Lodge.

The Impact of Freemasonry on the Secular and Liberal Discourse in Mexico
by Guillermo De Los Reyes, Translated by Bradley L. Drew

In this thought-provoking book, De Los Reyes argues that Freemasonry, through its lodges, played a decisive role in shaping Mexico's national thought, contributing to the creation of a liberal and secular State and fostering anticlerical sentiments among the laity that endured well into the twentieth century.

The French Rite: Enlightenment Culture
Cécile Révauger, Editor

This book, focused on the French Rite, covers the founding principles of the Enlightenment and their influence on the birth of modern Freemasonry as we know it today. The authors revisit the fundamental values of the Enlightenment, from a rational approach to religious tolerance and cosmopolitanism.

The Great Transformation: Scottish Freemasonry 1725-1810
by Dr. Mark C. Wallace

This book examines Scottish Freemasonry in its wider British and European contexts between the years 1725 and 1810. The Enlightenment effectively crafted the modern mason and propelled Freemasonry into a new era marked by growing membership and the creation of the Grand Lodge of Scotland.

Getting the Third Degree: Fraternalism, Freemasonry and History
Edited by Guillermo De Los Reyes and Paul Rich

As this engaging collection demonstrates, the doors being opened on the subject range from art history to political science to anthropology, as well as gender studies, sociology and more. The organizations discussed may insist on secrecy, but the research into them belies that.

Freemasonry: A French View
by Roger Dachez and Alain Bauer

Perhaps one should speak not of Freemasonry but of Freemasonries in the plural. In each country Masonic historiography has developed uniqueness. Two of the best known French Masonic scholars present their own view of the worldwide evolution and challenging mysteries of the fraternity over the centuries.

Worlds of Print: The Moral Imagination of an Informed Citizenry, 1734 to 1839
by John Slifko

John Slifko argues that freemasonry was representative and played an important role in a larger cultural transformation of literacy and helped articulate the moral imagination of an informed democratic citizenry via fast emerging worlds of print.

Why Thirty-Three?: Searching for Masonic Origins
by S. Brent Morris, PhD

What "high degrees" were in the United States before 1830? What were the activities of the Order of the Royal Secret, the precursor of the Scottish Rite? A complex organization with a lengthy pedigree like Freemasonry has many basic foundational questions waiting to be answered, and that's what this book does: answers questions.

A Place in the Lodge: Dr. Rob Morris, Freemasonry and the Order of the Eastern Star
by Nancy Stearns Theiss, PhD

Ridiculed as "petticoat masonry," critics of the Order of the Eastern Star did not deter Rob Morris' goal to establish a Masonic organization that included women as members. Morris carried the ideals of Freemasonry through a despairing time of American history.

Brought to Light: The Mysterious George Washington Masonic Cave
by Jason Williams MD

The George Washington Masonic Cave near Charles Town, West Virginia, contains a signature carving of George Washington dated 1748. This book painstakingly pieces together the chronicled events and real estate archives related to the cavern in order to sort out fact from fiction.

Dudley Wright: Writer, Truthseeker & Freemason
by John Belton

Dudley Wright (1868-1950) was an Englishman and professional journalist who took a universalist approach to the various great Truths of Life. He travelled though many religions in his life and wrote about them all, but was probably most at home with Islam.

History of the Grand Orient of Italy
Emanuela Locci, Editor

No book in Masonic literature upon the history of Italian Freemasonry has been edited in English up to now. This work consists of eight studies, covering a span from the Eighteenth Century to the end of the WWII, tracing through the story, the events and pursuits related to the Grand Orient of Italy.

westphaliapress.org

www.ingramcontent.com/pod-product-compliance
Lightning Source LLC
Chambersburg PA
CBHW052135070526
44585CB00017B/1838